IMAGES OF WAR
THE ROYAL ARMOURED CORPS IN THE COLD WAR 1946–1990

We dedicate this work to all who served as volunteers or as National Servicemen in the Royal Armoured Corps during the Cold War, and to all attached REME personnel who served alongside them. It should never be forgotten that the Royal Armoured Corps lost many brave men through the forty-five years covered in this study, both in action and in training. This book is also dedicated to their memory.

IMAGES OF WAR
THE ROYAL ARMOURED CORPS IN THE COLD WAR 1946–1990

RARE PHOTOGRAPHS FROM WARTIME ARCHIVES

M P ROBINSON AND ROB GRIFFIN

Pen & Sword
MILITARY

First published in Great Britain in 2016 by
PEN & SWORD MILITARY
an imprint of
Pen & Sword Books Ltd,
47 Church Street, Barnsley,
South Yorkshire.
S70 2AS

ISBN 978-1-47384-375-2

Typeset by Mac Style Ltd, Bridlington, East Yorkshire
Printed and bound by CPI Group (UK) Ltd, Croydon, CR0 4YY

Pen & Sword Books Ltd incorporates the imprints of
Pen & Sword Aviation, Pen & Sword Family History, Pen & Sword Maritime,
Pen & Sword Military, Pen & Sword Discovery, Wharncliffe Local History,
Wharncliffe True Crime, Wharncliffe Transport, Pen and Sword Select,
Pen and Sword Military Classics

For a complete list of Pen & Sword titles please contact:
PEN & SWORD BOOKS LIMITED
47 Church Street, Barnsley, South Yorkshire, S70 2AS, England.
E-mail: enquiries@pen-and-sword.co.uk
Website: www.pen-and-sword.co.uk

Contents

Acknowledgements

The authors express their thanks to Liam Robinson for his help preparing this book, to Chris Robinson and Matt Jones for their editing and to Henry Wilson for his patience, support and guidance. We would like to thank the following gentlemen for their help, for sharing their experiences, and for supporting this project through a long genesis. Without their kindness, this book would never have been possible.

Special thanks to Major-General Sir Laurence New, CB, CBE, and to the 4th and 7th RTR History website, and to Tom Coates, to the late Jim Smith, to Barrie Dady, John K. Webster and Gary Rathke of the 3rd Carabiniers Association, to Brigadier Johnny Torrens-Spence CBE, and Lieutenant-Colonel Noel McCleery OBE of the Royal Dragoon Guards Association, to Richard Allen, Malcolm Cleverley, Pete Dobson, Terry Denton, Brian Simpson, Brian Clarke, Dorian Llewelyn, Lieutenant-Colonel Dick Taylor, Fred Peall, Rob Jacobs, Peter Hill, Andy Hill, Peter Smith, A. Crowder, Jumbo Harrison, Justin Steadman, Duncan McKenzie, Harry Woods, Keith Frape, Lawrence Skuse, D.H. Wright, John Jollivet, Bob Girling, Charlie Welchman, Pim Hogben and the Lancers Media Group, Geoffrey Wells, Johnnie Rose, Peter Brown, Mark Hayward, Lieutenant-Colonel Michael Rose, Simon Dunstan, Steven Zaloga, Gary Elmes, Keith Paget, Paul Bethany, Brian Harrington-Spier, Boris Mollo, Johnathon Godfrey, Patrick Baty, Peter Robinson, Tim Strickland, Shane Lovell, Ivor Pollington, and Meyrick Griffith-Jones.

M.P. Robinson also thanks his wife Nisa, and his children Leif, Owyn, Alexandria, Griffin and Thor for their understanding throughout the preparation of this book.

Dedication

We dedicate this work to all who served as volunteers or as National Servicemen in the Royal Armoured Corps during the Cold War, and to all attached REME personnel who served alongside them. It should never be forgotten that the Royal Armoured Corps lost many brave men through the forty-five years covered in this study, both in action and in training. This book is also dedicated to their memory.

Introduction

This book is a brief survey of a broad subject and describes the Royal Armoured Corps (RAC) during the forty-five tense years after the Second World War. For most who were armoured vehicle crewmen in this period it will be remembered with some degree of nostalgia. For those looking upon this period for the first time, the material in this book gives a glimpse at the way of life in the Cold War era Royal Armoured Corps. Over the five decades covered, a great deal changed within the Corps and in the world at large. The British Army changed, and Britain herself changed beyond all recognition. The previous titles that cover this period of the Corps' history and various regimental journals were heavily consulted as references for this work. Major Kenneth Macksey MC and Lieutenant-Colonel George Forty OBE both wrote valuable research into the RAC and the Royal Tank Regiment which has formed an excellent basis for this study. We have also relied on the memoirs of soldiers who served in the Corps. In this age of internet, old comrades' organizations have found a new vitality and this mode of communication greatly facilitated researching this book. The authors have benefited from the generosity of many former soldiers of the RAC.

The RAC withered immediately after the Second World War, grew in the 1950s to its largest peacetime size and then shrank again with the rest of the army as budgets dictated. This book includes period photographs, most seen here for the first time, from the personal collections of its veterans. Every time the Corps was reduced in size from 1957 until the end of the Cold War it retained all the responsibilities of a larger force. Defending West Germany, in Asian jungles, in the deserts of the Middle East, in Northern Ireland or thundering across Canadian prairies, the men of the RAC served their sovereign and nation. This book cannot tell the story of every regiment or that of every station manned by the RAC. It touches on the larger events in the forty-five years after the Second World War and we hope it encourages the in-depth study of all RAC regiments. It is a humble tribute to all who have served in the Royal Armoured Corps – an organization that continues to evolve in the face of many challenges and still carries its responsibilities with the greatest professionalism.

The end of the Second World War, and the start of a new era. A group of recruits from one of the Training Regiments RAC photographed seated on a Churchill Mk.VII in 1946 at Lulworth. The Churchill is probably a vehicle returned from the continent, and exhibits repaired battle damage on the turret side. (*Brian Simpson*)

Trooper Peter Smith, 3rd Hussars, seen in typical working uniform overalls in 1956. The uniform had changed very little since 1945 and the cotton overalls worn in summer and 'pixie suit' worn in winter will be remembered to RAC men of the 1950s and 1960s. (*Peter Smith*)

Crews of the 17th/21st Lancers at rest in long grass during an exercise in 1951. A camouflaged Centurion can be seen in the background. The men wear a mixture of khaki and camouflage denim tank suits, and pixie suits. (*T. Denton*)

The life in an armoured regiment was not all about vehicle maintenance and preparing for war. A soldier might find himself assigned to any range of tasks, exciting or mundane. Trooper Tom Coates of the 3rd Carabiniers is seen here while assigned to driving around a Brigade Major RAC. (*T. Coates*)

Some of the turret crew of a 9th/12th Lancers Centurion Mk.13 seen in 1967 during a break in a summer training period in West Germany. (*Brian Clarke*)

A tank commander salutes while passing a saluting base emblazoned with Union Flags in 1952. This Centurion belonged to the 17th/21st Lancers and the occasion was the Queen's first birthday spent as a reigning sovereign. At this time the mailed fist was the emblem of the 6th Armoured Division, newly raised for service in West Germany. (*T. Denton*)

This group of troopers, NCOs and officers were photographed in the 1950s and show a variety of uniforms in use by RAC personnel at the time. A mixture of wartime and postwar battledress, Denison smocks and pixie suits are seen here. We can just about make out the cap badge of the Royal Horse Guards on some of the figures, so it may be from the period 1951–52 during the reconstitution of the 11th Armoured Division. It is very likely that many of these men were National Service conscripts. (*M.P. Robinson Collection with thanks to Dick Taylor*)

6th RTR Troopers boarding a plane for home in 1958. The 1950s were the first time that soldiers were moved in significant numbers by air, and they travelled armed in the those days. (*Pete Dobson*)

Chapter One

The Early Post-War Period

The Royal Armoured Corps (or RAC) was formed on the eve of war in 1939 from the battalions of the Royal Tank Corps and the mechanised regiments of cavalry. Six bloody years later the Axis lay defeated and Britain stood exhausted from campaigns fought around the globe. The army faced occupation duties in Europe, and the unpredictable burdens of keeping the peace in a far-flung empire. In August 1945 the British Army of the Rhine (BAOR) was

The 1st Royal Tank Regiment on parade in Germany after the end of the war in Europe. The wartime RTR was a huge organization with twelve regular regiments and many other units raised for the duration. Some of these quickly disbanded RTR regiments returned as Territorial regiments in 1947. (*MP Robinson Collection*)

In 1947 the 13th/18th Hussars had some M24 Chaffee tanks on strength as well as armoured cars. During the winter of 1947, food and fuel shortages were the cause of some unrest in the local population. The tanks were eventually handed over to the 14th/20th Hussars, and the 13th/18th Hussars spent the remaining months of their occupation duty equipped with armoured cars. (John Jollivet)

reformed from the British occupation forces in northwest Germany. BAOR was to remain a constant factor for the RAC for most of the next fifty years. Outside of Europe, North Africa, India, Palestine, and Malaya had RAC units present in their army garrisons as well. The RAC's composition was unique in that it included the army's oldest cavalry regiments and the battalions of the Royal Tank Regiment, which dated only from the First World War. Old cavalry regiments with officers traditionally connected to the British establishment had throughout the Second World War been brigaded with the very junior units of the Royal Tank Regiment. The Royal Armoured Corps had some of Britain's best military minds in its officer corps, veteran commanders to lead the corps united through the turbulent peace. Many career officers in the Royal Armoured Corps had found themselves in the few years after the war's end with stark choices. Wartime regimental commanders often accepted lower rank to stay in the shrinking army, or left the service. A rapid turn-over of officers and NCOs came as wartime regiments disbanded and as the Python leave system took effect. In the next two years the number of available junior officers dwindled sharply in the entire army, creating a shortage of troop leaders in the RAC which was eventually resolved by conscription.[1]

Attlee's government wanted to reduce the army and the size of the empire quickly. In late 1945 the army disbanded the Royal Reconnaissance Corps, the wartime RAC regiments raised from converted infantry regiments, and the territorial RTR regiments. Most of these

Two Humber scout cars of the 13th/18th Hussars parked at the barracks at Wolfenbuttel in 1946 or 1947. Also pictured in the background are a Daimler Armoured Car and one of the Chaffees. The 13th/18th Hussars finished the war with the 8th Armoured Brigade on Shermans, but within a year they were under orders of the 5th Infantry Division on armoured cars, with only enough men to form two squadrons. (*John Jollivet*)

units had finished the war overseas – mainly in Italy, the Middle East, India or northern Europe. The rapid disbandment of these units led to some administrative difficulties and to the assignment of occupation duties throughout Europe to the remaining RAC regiments on the continent. In the last months of 1945 and for much of 1946 there was a whirlwind of personnel changes in the individual regiments, and many unit movements. The armoured units in the 8th Army and the 21st Army Group became widely dispersed across Western Europe in the course of occupation duties.

Occupation was very different from wartime armoured or reconnaissance operations. Regiments detached into squadrons in order to control large areas. Many regiments exchanged some (or all) of their tanks for armoured cars. Individual troops patrolled, hunting for caches of weapons and rounding up persons of interest. Temporary camps were set up – often in former enemy barracks. Wartime soldiers departed in a steady stream, and numbers were made up from disbanded regiments as an expedient. Even this didn't provide enough men for long, and many units manned only two of their sabre squadrons by the middle months of 1946. In the regiments themselves, time not spent on showing the flag or assisting displaced people was spent on honing peacetime skills or in sports. Bases were moved repeatedly, and it became hard to track changes in assignment as larger formations disappeared and areas returned to civil administration.[2]

A Comet of the 2nd Queen's Bays about to test its ditch crossing ability in Italy in 1946. The Bays were then part of the 2nd Armoured Brigade, 1st Armoured Division (along with the 4th RTR, 6th RTR and 9th Lancers). The 2nd Armoured Brigade's role in the area was to dissuade Tito's forces from attempting to advance into Trieste. The potential for violence was real; the British commander of the Pola district was assassinated by an Italian fascist in protest to the handover of Istria to the Yugoslavs in 1947. The Bays left Italy for Egypt in June 1947. (*Brian Simpson*)

The RAC in time of peace was controlled by the Director, Royal Armoured Corps (DRAC), and by the War Office, and they both needed to balance the needs of the army with those of the peacetime budget. The first post-war RAC Conference was held in late 1945. The RAC's senior officers and the War Office both made a concerted effort to determine the best ways to implement the structural lessons of the war while reducing the corps to a manageable size. The RAC's peacetime strength was set at twenty cavalry regiments and eight RTR regiments. Not everyone saw a rapid force reduction as a sensible move for British interests. At the 1946 Royal Armoured Corps conference Field-Marshal Montgomery himself argued that Britain's future security required a large post-war professional regular army backed by a large citizen reserve army. He proposed that Britain kept a regular army of two armoured divisions and four infantry divisions, with three additional independent armoured brigades. He envisioned a requirement for four RAC reconnaissance regiments for the regular infantry divisions, and four armoured car regiments as army troops. This force was to be manned by conscripts and by a smaller core of regulars. Monty's ideal regular army was backed up by a Territorial Army of two armoured divisions, three armoured brigades, seven RAC reconnaissance regiments

A Comet in course of a gearbox change during the Queen's Bays service in Palmanova, Italy in 1946. The Comet was generally a quick, reliable and maneuverable vehicle. In Libya drivers occasionally raced them for fun – a strictly unofficial pastime! (*Brian Simpson*)

(for seven infantry divisions) and four armoured car regiments. It would have been an army almost on a wartime scale.[3]

If combined with new equipment, Montgomery's proposal would have provided a strong force for intervention in Europe. He saw that the United States and Great Britain needed to keep large standing armies to discourage Soviet expansion westwards. Monty's vision ran against both the current of political thought and the economic realities of setting up a welfare state, but he could have had a crystal ball for the accuracy of his estimation of the army's needs... and of what was to come. The west had much to mistrust in the USSR's post-war policies. The reality was that the RAC needed to simultaneously shrink and modernise, in order to protect British interests at an acceptable cost. Shrink it did – at a rapid pace. By late 1946 the British Army in Europe had dwindled to three under-strength corps. By the end of the year the 7th Armoured Division was all that remained of the wartime armoured divisions, as the 11th had disbanded during the year. BAOR was reduced to a peacekeeping force for the next two years as Great Britain cast her eyes at her shrinking empire.

By 1947 only three nominal divisions remained in the areas under British control in Europe. Some regiments returning to Britain after years abroad were immediately redeployed as conflicts flared in Palestine and India. The regiments in the Middle East were stationed in Palestine, Egypt and Libya – in tanks and armoured cars. The Suez Canal, the main strategic concern in the area, was guarded on both the eastern and western sides by RAC units. There was a real risk of war with Jewish and Egyptian forces while Israel was established. As a result of misidentification Egyptian forces on several occasions opened fire on British armoured units on exercises in the eastern Sinai in 1946. The important areas where armoured forces were still deployed were all outside Europe – and all were associated to the strategic needs

Comet T-335919 with fitters sitting on the engine deck in the workshop area of the Bays' tank park in Fanara, Egypt in 1947. The Comet was a good vehicle for its time and replaced most of the British Shermans after the war. The Bays moved to Palestine, Egypt and Libya in 1947 and finally returned to England in October 1947. (*Brian Simpson*)

of the empire. Five regiments were still in India, and eight were serving in the Middle East (half of whom were equipped with armoured cars). Smaller detachments were located in Hong Kong and Japan. The 4th RTR was sent to Palestine in 1948 equipped with Comet tanks to protect the final British withdrawal from Israeli attacks. In Malaya, where communist agitation had been a threat since 1945, the 3rd RTR had a small presence (with the bulk of the regiment stationed in Hong Kong). In the same year the 4th Hussars joined them on a three year assignment in armoured cars as the situation in the colony became more serious.

Two Bays Comets at Fanara, Egypt, 1947. The armoured regiments abroad in the years immediately after the war mostly received Cromwell and Comet tanks, although the Sherman was retained by units in India until they returned to the United Kingdom. (*Brian Simpson*)

A Bays Comet at Fanara, Egypt in 1947. The Comet was only used in North West Europe during the war but saw worldwide service thereafter. (*Brian Simpson*)

It became impossible to keep a large enough force to intervene in Europe after 1946 while the army's budget shrank and its numbers dwindled. During this period the RAC's BAOR commitment was a weak force of six armoured regiments, which represented the only full strength regiments in the corps. For the five years leading up to the Korean War, manpower resources were pulled in so many directions that the supply of men could not keep pace with the British Army's needs. The RAC was doomed to suffer from manpower shortages with the rest of the army. The government and the General Staff were aware of the need to re-equip, but the process had a slow start while larger issues were addressed. Prime Minister Attlee's government broke with established traditions by creating a separate Ministry of Defence in 1947. This was significant because the Prime Minister had usually combined the Defence Minister's portfolio with his own, although the War Office continued to dictate military policy. The simplification of controlling the army was a positive move that made decision making more efficient. The Royal Armoured Corps also rationalised its establishment, improving administrative functions at its Bovington Centre.

The Labour government introduced National Service, as a military conscription period of eighteen months; this lasted until 1960. National Service changed the character of the Royal Armoured Corps and resulted in its sudden expansion. During the war designated training regiments supplied trained recruits to the RAC and this system continued with the 65th, 66th, 67th and 68th Training Regiments, who trained new intakes for the first years of National Service. The corps eventually met its manpower needs with national servicemen, many of whom became excellent soldiers. Officers could not be produced as quickly. The War Office, in response to its large losses of officers to demobilisation, revised its Army Reserve of Officers in 1948. It invited reserve officers to join either the Regular Army Reserve of Officers or the Army Officers Emergency Reserve. It also invited former officers with less than ten years of service, or officers who had taken wartime emergency commissions (and former officers of the Indian Army), to join the Territorial Army or the regular and emergency

Staghounds served the same role in Italy that the Daimler armoured cars performed in armoured car regiments in North West Europe during the war. It remained in service for a few years after the war with the British Army. Occupation duties like patrolling road networks were much easier with armoured cars than with tanks. Trooper Taffy Evans of the 1st King's Dragoon Guards, with Staghound No.116308 (*Fairway*) in Muquibila, Palestine 1946. (*Brian Simpson*)

reserves. These measures were necessary because the army by 1948 had too few junior officers to deal with National Service.[4]

At loggerheads with sudden growth of the citizen army was the tiny size of the regular army force available to train them in the late 1940s. With limited manpower in most regiments, taking on and training new conscripts at first caused grave difficulties. The increased training needs of the National Service conscripts were handled by the rationalization of the Royal Armoured Corps training establishment into three sites using the wartime format and training regiments. The main training bases were at Catterick, Carlisle and Barnard Castle (which trained armoured car crews exclusively). The biggest training areas for armoured regiments in the UK were dotted around Salisbury Plain, and the infantry school at Warminster was permanent home to a detached armoured squadron. Providing instructors to these establishments caused a regular drain on manpower for the RAC's regiments in the United Kingdom.

The second drain on the home based armoured regiments was the assignment of some regiments based in Britain to train the Territorial Army's RAC-affiliated regiments in 1947. National Service required fifty-four months of reserve service in the TA after full time regimental service in the army. The permanent staff for each of newly raised territorial regiments came from the associated regular RAC regiment. The withdrawal of troops from India and Palestine by the end of 1948 would have resulted in the wholescale disbandment of more RAC units had training needs not been so pressing. Most RAC units tasked with training had only been back in the UK for a short time, and all were below strength.[5]

A few Alectos were used overseas with armoured regiments in the Middle East and Italy after the war. The tarpaulin in this photo is to keep the gun breech dust-free. (*Brian Simpson*)

The Daimler Dingo Scout Car was retained in service after the war until the late 1950s. In postwar armoured regiments both the Dingo and the wartime Humber were used for liaison purposes; these examples belong to the Queen's Bays. In this 1947 photo taken in Egypt the vehicles are marked as belonging to the senior regiment in the 1st Armoured Division. (*Brian Simpson*)

A Cromwell Mk.VIII of the 3rd/4th County of London Yeomanry in the 1950s. The Territorial Army's RAC regiments numbered over thirty between 1947 and 1961, and in 1947–1948 the number of units requiring permanent staff from the regular Royal Armoured Corps regiments (themselves short of manpower) put severe strain on the corps. Eventually, the needs of the TA units were met by the influx of former conscripts. After 1961, the number of TA units was steadily reduced and the TA's armoured formations disappeared. The 3rd/4th CLY was part of the 56th (City of London) Armoured Division, TA. (*The Kent and Sharpshooters Yeomanry Museum*)

With the exception of the strategic reserve, these regiments were stationed on a mixture of established camps, or reoccupied decrepit wartime bases that had been vacated for two years. The regular RAC regiments assigned to training the part time soldiers did, by all accounts, an excellent job, but the price was high until the regular RAC regiments were up to their own manpower requirement. With detached squadrons spread around the country, RAC units training the TA fell below operational capability very quickly. The Queen's Bays, the 12th Lancers, the 14th/20th Hussars, the 8th Royal Tank Regiment and the 17th/21st Lancers all served as training units in 1948. The other repatriated armoured regiments dedicated to training the Territorial Army at various times soon included the 3rd Carabiniers, the 1st Kings's Dragoon Guards, the Life Guards, the 7th Hussars, the 8th Hussars, the 9th Lancers, the 2nd RTR and the 6th RTR. With the exception of the six regiments in BAOR, every regiment in the Royal Armoured Corps was well under strength. Poor equipment maintenance capabilities in the dispersed armoured squadrons quickly reduced vehicle availability, and inadequate accommodation in disused wartime camps added misery to boredom.[6]

The 1947 journal of the 3rd Carabiniers (who had just returned to England after ten years in India and who had taken up garrison at Bordon and Perham Down near Tidworth) mentioned their unfortunate conditions:

Westminster Dragoons clad in windproof smocks with a Daimler Armoured Car Mk.I around 1959. Armoured car units of the Territorial Army continued to resemble late wartime troops until the early 1960s as a result of the preponderance of wartime equipment, including Scammel Pioneer recovery tractors. (*D.H. Wright*)

'In our review of 1946, we could tell of demonstrations and exercises with full scales of equipment; this year we have been kept drastically short of both men and vehicles.'[7]

For such troops back from the Middle and Far East, the complaint was familiar, and made for a very anticlimactic return home.

The Berlin Crisis slowed the plans for reducing the size of the peacetime RAC and the Middle East remained a British strategic priority. The 1st Armoured Division (and later the 10th Armoured Division) based in Egypt and Libya became the scene for a local military build-up. The Malayan emergency flared to greater intensity during 1948 and lasted twelve years. In late 1950, the 13th/18th Hussars served in Malaya in armoured cars with a small tank detachment from 3rd Royal Tank Regiment. Although it only required a few RAC regiments at any time, the war in Malaya was fought in jungles defending British-owned mines and rubber plantations. At first vehicles dating back to the Second World War were used against the Malayan communists, who had relatively few antitank weapons beyond landmines. For RAC troopers, much of the Malayan emergency was spent in support of patrols or protecting convoys from ambush.

On the ranges with the Westminster Dragoons in the late 1950s, this Daimler has a range flag flying (probably a green one indicating that all weapons are unloaded) and instructors present. The most serious training was conducted at annual camps. (*D.H. Wright*)

The Daimler Armoured Car Mk.I was armed with a 2-pdr gun with fifty-two rounds, had four-wheel drive with a road speed of 50 mph, and carried a crew of three men. This example was with the Westminster Dragoons in 1959. (*D.H. Wright*)

Digging out a bogged down Westminster Dragoons Daimler Armoured Car. (*D.H. Wright*)

The territorials, like the rest of the RAC, used halftracks for many years after the war. They were used as APCs, command vehicles and as fitters' vehicles. This one served in the Westminster Dragoons although its purpose is hard to tell with the tarpaulin fitted. (*D.H. Wright*)

The Westminster Dragoons were equipped with armoured cars in the 1950s, like the Daimler Armoured Car Mk.1s and Daimler Dingos seen here. Each troop in the sabre squadrons would have been equipped with two Dingoes and two Daimler Armoured Cars. The squadron heavy troop would have had four AEC Mk.III armoured cars, and the assault troop would have had White Scout Cars, halftracks or CT15s, but the Saladin and Saracen replaced these respectively at the end of the 1950s and in the early 1960s. (*D.H. Wright*)

It was fortunate that colonial actions could be conducted with old equipment against enemies who had no sophisticated antitank weapons. The Royal Armoured Corps was short of modern equipment at the end of the Second World War. The armoured regiments outside of BAOR and Britain sometimes used the leftover wartime equipment. In 1947 for example, the 4th/7th Dragoon Guards in Libya, were equipped with the obsolescent Cromwell cruiser tank. In 1951 these were handed back and newer Comets were received, but they were accompanied by the Archer SP 17-pounder. The Archer moved at less than 20 mph and fired (at the halt) rearwards over the engine decks. Each squadron had two troops of these incompatible and mismatched vehicles. Outside of Germany an amalgam of equipment was common. The unwritten rule for the next decade became that the regiments in Germany were equipped with new equipment first. As late as the middle 1950s, wartime machines stayed in service, especially with regiments in Britain and in the colonies. It took a good ten years to re-equip the Royal Armoured Corps with modern weapons.[8]

It was not just budgets that kept wartime equipment around in the late 1940s. The option of using American equipment had passed in 1945, and the army expected to buy British armoured fighting vehicles. The RAC's desire for first class equipment was often at odds with what was on offer. It was the job of the Director Royal Armoured Corps to ensure that the best available weapons were developed for and adopted by the RAC. While the small budget and the lack of decent designs prevented re-equipment old weapons had to suffice. British efforts at producing a world class battle tank design after the war very nearly came off the

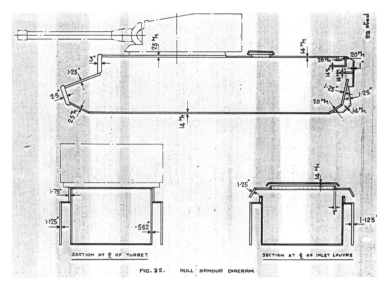

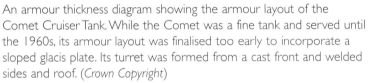

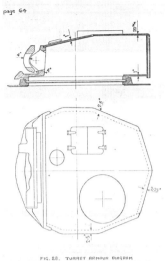

An armour thickness diagram showing the armour layout of the Comet Cruiser Tank. While the Comet was a fine tank and served until the 1960s, its armour layout was finalised too early to incorporate a sloped glacis plate. Its turret was formed from a cast front and welded sides and roof. (*Crown Copyright*)

The Comet turret was constructed similarly to the A41 and Centurion Mk.1 and mounted a powerful and accurate 77mm gun (*Crown Copyright*)

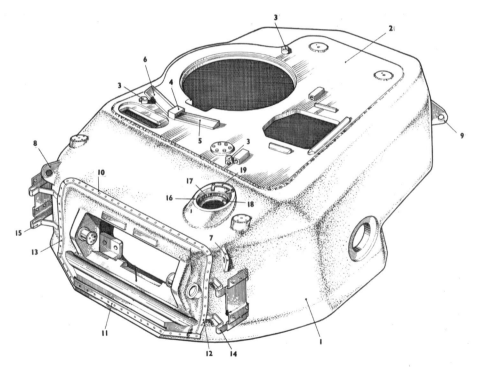

A late pattern Centurion Mk.3 turret casting. The Centurion turret underwent many detail changes between the original cast Centurion Mk.2 turret and the final production Mk.10 turret with the metalastic mantlet, but the general layout remained the same. It had a 152mm thick face and 90mm sides and rear. (*Crown Copyright*)

rails. The Tortoise assault tank and Black Prince heavy infantry tank of 1946 were both designs that ignored wartime lessons, but both were seriously evaluated after the war was over. Attempts to design a new light tank were equally unsuccessful. Designers (it seemed) were suffering from a hangover from the wartime days where private industry regularly attempted to call the tune, and design efforts lacked enough official direction.[9]

The one enduring exception was the A41 which entered a limited production run of prototypes at the end of 1944. The first six were rushed to Germany in *Operation Sentry* in order to gain combat experience, but arrived after the surrender. Changes to the design were demanded, but the A41 showed promise as the RAC's post-war medium tank. It was Britain's first tank with a sloped glacis plate and employed the proven Rolls Royce Meteor engine. This tank became the iconic Centurion, and the first hundred were ordered in 1946. The second production version with the definitive cast turret was ordered later that year. The new Centurion Mk.1 and Mk.2 mounted the 17-pounder gun, but it was doubted that it could remain competitive against Soviet designs for very long. The German Pak 43 8.8cm gun was the best tank gun devised by any wartime combatant and was studied after the war to develop

The M10c served in the Royal Artillery between 1944 and 1946 and thereafter until the mid-1950s in divisional RAC regiments. It was also used in the Territorial Army RAC regiments. It was a well-designed conversion of the American Lend-Lease M10 mounting the British 17-pounder gun. The M10c was sometimes known as the Achilles, although this name seemed to have been used more commonly after 1945. The vehicles seen here were on display at Bovington in the late 1950s. (*Crown Copyright*)

the new 84.3mm Q.F. 20-pounder gun. The RAC hoped this would match any potential enemy's fire power. While the first Centurions were finally leaving the factories, the War Office had already decided that a better tank was wanted. They ordered the development of a new family of tanks estimated to be far superior to anything yet fielded by the RAC, a 'Universal Tank'.

Early post war tank design suffered from a dilution of efforts. Part of the problem was that the development of armoured fighting vehicles still took place under the wartime jurisdiction divided between the Ministry of Supply and the War Office. In 1947 the British Government established the Fighting Vehicle Research and Development Establishment (FVRDE) at Chertsey, Surrey. This was a significant effort by the government to streamline military vehicle design into one establishment. It was hoped that FVRDE would coordinate the army's needs with the Royal Ordnance factories and with the private industries that built armoured fighting vehicles. Control of existing tank designs was handed over to FVRDE, including the further development of the Centurion. The early days at FVRDE seem to have been spent fixing much that was not broken, but in fairness the new establishment inherited ongoing projects with significant investments already made. The proposed A45 of 1946 was one of its first projects and lacked the focus of later programmes. It was supposed to be the replacement for all the tank types left in service in the Royal Armoured Corps, including the Centurion. The A45 was

The third A41 prototype. Developed as a heavy cruiser tank, the A41 formed the basis of the Centurion design and was ordered with numerous detail differences in a run of twenty prototypes. Six of these were sent to Germany for field testing in April 1945, but late deliveries resulted in them missing the war. The 20mm Polsten secondary armament was not adopted for the production Centurion Mk.1. (*Crown Copyright*)

The rear view of an A41 shows the familiar Centurion lines – the reinforced engine deck was quickly discarded once the 20-Pdr was adopted in order to save weight. (*Crown Copyright*)

The Tortoise was another dead end in AFV design that was conceived as an assault tank for breaking the Siegfried line. The end product was not ready for evaluation until 1946. The six turretless prototypes then underwent extensive mobility and gunnery trials but a production order was never seriously considered. They mounted an impressive 32-pounder gun and proved to be surprisingly nimble vehicles for all of their 78 tons. (*Crown Copyright*)

The A43 Black Prince was a Vauxhall design that perpetuated the Churchill's construction principles which might have been a valuable weapon had it been ready in 1943. By postwar standards it was an anachronism but, due to Vauxhall's political connections, it was seriously considered for production in the year after the war. (*Crown Copyright*)

also supposed to form the basis for a large range of specialist vehicles. FVRDE renumbered the A45 specification FV201, and its armament was expected to be the new QF 20-pounder.

The FV201 of 1948, despite its well-intentioned design, failed to deliver any improvements on the Centurion. While officers, boffins and engineers mulled over what was actually wanted from the FV201 design over the next year, East-West relations worsened. The only modern tanks on strength were in the 7th Armoured Division in Germany. The Centurions had only arrived in BAOR in 1947 and all other regiments had wartime equipment. This added urgency to the Universal Tank project but also drove Centurion development because it was already in production. In 1949 the FV201 was re-evaluated by the RAC's senior officers and when the 20-pounder proved to fit in the Centurion, the Universal Tank was cancelled. Thereafter, the RAC did not consider adopting families of heavy fighting vehicles designed by committees. It was the final break with the wartime tank design legacy.[10]

Having such an excellent basic design as the Centurion in production in 1948 was fortunate for the RAC. It proved an excellent tank, almost in spite of the War Office who had already thought so hard about replacing it. Procuring sufficient new tanks to equip the Royal Armoured Corps wholesale was another matter, and few Centurions could be afforded. The post-war army budget was small and the national economy staggered under the burden of reconstruction. Large scale production of the Centurion Mk.3 only began under the renewed threat of war in 1949, and only after large export orders were received. In the meantime the older Comet was issued in numbers but production had ended in 1945, so other wartime vehicles also remained in service. The 8th Hussars and 1st Royal Tank Regiment, amongst the

FV 201.

PROVISIONAL PICTORIAL SKETCH.

A sketch of the A45, which reached the prototype stage in 1946 and which was hoped to offer more than the Centurion. The A45 was cancelled in 1949 because it offered no real advantages over the tank it was supposed to succeed. Its hull went on to be developed for the FV214 Conqueror a few years later. (*Private Collection*)

very first units to equip with the Centurion Mk.3, only received their full complement of tanks in the autumn of 1950.[11]

The need for a collective Western European alliance was accepted in both Washington and London and the creation of the North Atlantic Treaty Organization (or NATO) followed in 1949. As a key component of Britain's contribution to NATO, the British Army of the Rhine grew from a modest occupation force into a fully armed corps. Great Britain took a leap of faith into continental European security and the army's strategic priorities were reoriented on the defence of West Germany. For the Royal Armoured Corps this became a lifeline for regiments under threat of disbandment. It also brought the manpower, training and equipment-related challenges associated with the need to grow again rapidly. The strength of 1st British Corps was to be based on conventional armoured divisions with all necessary supporting arms maintained at wartime establishment.

The importance of the armoured regiments in 1st British Corps cannot be overstated. Britain had no nuclear capability and the army had to rely on its conventional weapons. Each armoured division was organised, as in wartime, with an armoured reconnaissance regiment under divisional command and two constituent brigades. Of these one would be an armoured brigade of one hundred and fifty-six tanks in three armoured regiments, the other a motorised infantry brigade. Each armoured regiment had fifty-two battle tanks in three squadrons. 1st British Corps needed sixteen armoured regiments as soon as they could be raised to operate at war establishment. The four armoured divisions required in 1951 needed over seven

A Centurion of the 8th RTR in the late 1940s. After two years in Austria, Egypt and Palestine the 8th RTR served as a tank training regiment at Catterick between 1947 and 1951. Before its amalgamation in 1959 it then served in BAOR (*Private Collection*)

This Centurion Mk.2 T-451861 was photographed in 1948, possibly with the 17th/21st Lancers judging by the cap badge and probably therefore at Catterick. The Centurion Mk.2 carried a 17-pounder gun. When the Mk.3 was introduced in 1949, many Mk.2s were upgraded with the more powerful 20-pounder gun. (*MP Robinson Collection with thanks to Dick Taylor*)

A Centurion of the 17th/21st Lancers in 1952. The 17th/21st Lancers arrived in Germany in December 1951 after training in Britain. These Lancers are inspecting the tracks and topping up the oil levels in the axle arms of a Centurion Mk.3. We can see the new census system in use as well as the disruptive white paint applied to the underside of the gun barrel. (*T. Denton*)

German fitters replacing a Bays Centurion's front idler wheel in Germany in 1951. The idler wheel controlled track tension and required regular inspection and adjustment. (*Brian Simpson*)

This Centurion Mk.3 of C Squadron, 17th/21st Lancers lost a track during training in the Munster area, West Germany in 1952. It is no doubt waiting for the squadron LAD and their venerable Churchill ARV Mk.II, a vehicle barely capable of recovering a fifty ton tank. The 49 arm of service number indicates the HQ of an armoured brigade. This is a late production Mk.3 with the gun removal hatch deleted from the rear of the turret casting. (*T. Denton*)

Good Hope was built as a Centurion Mk.2 or as an early Centurion Mk.3 (and possibly a Mk.5 by the time of this photo if it had received the .30 Browning coaxial machinegun). Given the marking system, this tank could be with the 6th Armoured Division's 6th RTR in the 1952–1956 period or with the 14th/20th Hussars in the 20th Armoured Brigade after 1956. The repetition of the mailed fist emblem and the location of the tank name on the glacis are unusual. (*MP Robinson collection*)

Almost certainly painted in SCC15 Khaki Drab with black disruptive stripes, this later production Centurion Mk.3 belonged to No 1 Troop, C Squadron 17th/21st Lancers in 1952. In 1951 the 17th/21st Lancers moved to BAOR, where they joined the 20th Armoured Brigade of the 6th Armoured Division. (*T. Denton*)

hundred Centurions. In order to meet other contingencies in the Middle East and to keep a reserve in the UK, the number was expected to increase substantially. The RAC eventually adopted two types of tanks in BAOR in the 1950s. They were to be used in conjunction with each other in the same units. The Medium Gun Tank was by default the Centurion, and the vehicle that replaced the failed FV201 eventually became the Heavy Gun Tank in 1955. In the meantime the RAC finally had the promise of enough Centurions, new recruits and the resources to accomplish its mission.[12]

Chapter Two

Joining the Royal Armoured Corps

Troopers could volunteer or find themselves conscripted into the Royal Armoured Corps between the late 1940s and 1960. The national serviceman was assigned to his regiment based mostly on geographical location and education level. Most national servicemen went into the British Army and having passed strict medical selection were excellent quality manpower. The principal difference between volunteers and conscripts in the 1950s was the short duration of national service. National servicemen served in all major deployments (including Korea) in the frontline. About half of the Other Ranks in the British Army in the 1950s at any given time were conscripts, and the Royal Armoured Corps was no exception. There were also many

An Alecto at Lulworth in 1946 with trainee gun fitters. The Alecto was a self-propelled gun that was designed on the basis of the air portable Harry Hopkins light tank, adopted in small numbers as a reconnaissance vehicle after the war. (*Brian Simpson*)

volunteers and most of the officer and non-commissioned officer pool at any time consisted of regulars with varying years of service.

The volunteer had to be seventeen years of age and have parental consent to enlist (or seventeen and a half to sign up alone). He signed up at his local recruiting office specifying interest in the Royal Armoured Corps. A formal interview followed and upon successfully passing medical examination, he would swear an oath to serve Her Majesty the Queen for a given period. A nine year enlistment was often chosen, and many re-enlisted, though a shorter service could be selected. Within days of signing up the recruit entered a whole new life as he set off by train to Catterick.

Around 1949–1950, as National Service got into full stride, the duties of the training regiments encompassed the wholesale basic training of RAC recruits. Trade training was completed after the recruit had been posted to his regiment. The first stages of basic training lasted five weeks in the training regiment's A Squadron and began with drill, physical training and basic weapons training. This was a period of adjustment to army life and training was largely conducted under senior NCOs. Trade training in B Squadron was the second stage of training, in which the recruit would learn driving, gunnery or signalling (the wireless systems used in the various AFVs). These stages were normally both conducted at Catterick. The training instructors assessed the recruit's ability at the three trades over another six weeks to determine which suited the recruit, although every trooper mastered two of the three AFV crewman trades. After completing trade training (which could also entail assignment to other training centres like Lulworth), the new trooper moved to C Squadron to await posting to his new regiment.[13]

New troopers were sent by train, by ship or even by air to their regiments which were like families as much as institutions for making war. Recruits would complete their training in the image of their regiment over the next twelve months. This included troop training and vehicle crew training conducted by the regiment's instructors. The last years of a soldier's service might be spent as an instructor, often at Bovington, Lulworth or at Catterick with a training establishment or with the RAC Training Regiment.

The rapid growth of the early 1950s stretched the RAC. The army recognized the RAC as a key factor in the military build-up to ensure long-term security in Europe. BAOR garrisons grew out of wartime German barrack areas. The difference between a German barracks area and a base like Catterick (which in the 1950s still incorporated a large number of timber and corrugated huts) was glaring. Within a few years the bases in Germany had become permanent; NAAFI shops had all the amenities that a soldier and his family would need, and schools taught the base children just as they would have in Britain.[14]

Between 1952 and 1954, to avoid amalgamations, the Royal Armoured Corps replaced the permanent training regiments with a rotating two year assignment to each RAC regiment at Catterick. This was a distinct assignment and the training regiment formed part of the strategic reserve. The 5th Royal Inniskilling Dragoon Guards Journal of 1954 describes the complexity of processing new intakes upon their return from Korea and Egypt when they became the first regular regiment to assume the new role of Training Regiment RAC.

'The few categories of 'Trainee', 'Holdee' and 'Draftee' – soon to be lumped together by us under the good old fashioned title of 'Recruit' – were simplicity itself until we gradually discovered that they concealed no less than two dozen different types of military animal-tradesman and crewman; non-tradesman and specialist; officers, potential, cadet, 'deferred watch'; OR IV, potential and often non-potential; RPC recruits; CRMP recruits; PDC candidates; PEC candidates; RAEC probationers; relegates, retardees, medical discharges; transfers to other arms; under age Regulars – our biggest bane; and, last but not least, Band boys.'[15]

Peter Smith of the 3rd Hussars recalled:

'I had been a member of my school's Combined Cadet Force which was an advantage when it came to expressing one's preferences. I had left school at sixteen and was employed as a clerk so I was determined that I would do something quite different and applied for the Royal Armoured Corps. In due course I received a letter informing me that I was to report to the 5th Royal Inniskilling Dragoon Guards at Catterick! It should be explained that at that time (1955) tank and cavalry regiments took it in turns to be training regiments for the RAC as a whole. Near the end of the six-week basic training period we were all taken to a country pub by our sergeant where we enjoyed a pleasant, convivial drink together'.

The history of the 4th/7th Royal Dragoon Guards recounts training in detail between 1959 (when it took the job over from the 3rd Carabiniers) and 1962, when the job was handed over to the 3rd Royal Tank Regiment. In those brief two and half years the number of men in training each month grew from an average of four hundred recruits to some seven hundred. The surge in recruits was handled by drafting in some sixty-eight extra instructors from all over the RAC, many of them senior NCOs or soldiers finishing their enlistment period. The armoured car regiment and armoured regiment training were combined when the Barnard

The Boys Squadron RAC's instructor staff in the late 1950s, posed in front of the Bovington Tank Museum's Heavy Tank Mk.I. The wartime medals speak volumes for the military knowledge present in the group, which was drawn from most regiments in the Royal Armoured Corps. In the back row centre is Derek 'Spud' Taylor of the 9th Lancers, whose son Dick Taylor passed through the JLR in the 1970s and who was later commissioned. The Boys Squadron and Junior Leaders Regiment were vital parts of the RAC's recruiting system for much of the Cold War, but have sadly long disappeared. (*Dick Taylor*)

Castle training establishment closed after the 15th/19th Hussars departed in 1961. All of the RAC's training establishments were streamlined into a leaner and more centralised system at Catterick and wartime bases were closed.[16]

The RAC maintained a junior organization in the 1920s, and the Boys Squadron RAC was established in 1951 to revive this method of recruiting. It met with considerable success and expanded into a second squadron in 1954. By 1958 it became the Junior Leaders Regiment RAC (or JLR). The aim of the JLR was to provide training to future soldiers from the age of fifteen and a half with an education suitable to allow the boys a fast track into the NCO role. The JLR was based at Bovington Camp and taught a serious military trade curriculum with the usual subjects of mathematics, English, and history. It included a large music programme as an associated squadron also under the JLR umbrella. The JLR was composed of three squadrons and a passing out troop of prospective graduates, who entered the RAC regiments as trained crewmen. It was a solid start to life in the Royal Armoured Corps and many of the RAC's senior NCOs began their army life in the JLR prior to its disappearance in 1993.

Richard Allen of the 9/12th Lancers recalls:

'At fifteen years of age I either answered an advertisement or wrote a letter to the local Army Recruitment Office with a view to obtaining a few pamphlets on the life and

Gunners from the Junior Leaders Regiment in 1960 after a shoot at Lulworth on a Conqueror. Military education included large doses of hands-on trade training, and, in the case of these gunners, they were also reducing the Lulworth stockpile of 120mm ammunition which had grown too large! (*Dorian Llewellyn*)

weaponry of the Army. The army did not wait for me to wander into their recruiting office as is the norm today. One day whilst attending school, I was summoned to the Headmaster's Office where, waiting for me was a Recruiting Sergeant from the Northampton Recruiting Office. After a lengthy interview and question and answer session he informed me that I would be invited to the recruiting office in the near future for an assessment test, medical and possible attestation. At this time my elder brother had already enlisted and was serving with the Junior Leaders Regiment, Royal Armoured Corps.

'The Junior Leaders Regiment was run on a similar principle to a secondary school. The number of terms was dependent on your age at the time of enlistment. The younger you were, the more terms you served. The end result saw the young soldier transferring to a Regular Army Royal Armoured Corps regiment between the ages of seventeen and a half and eighteen. The JLR structure was similar to that of a Regular Army armoured regiment in that it was divided into four squadrons, A, B, C and HQ. All junior entrants were initially placed in either B or C Squadrons, in which the basic military skills and educational training took place. Having completed the required length of time in the junior squadrons, the aspiring soldier would be transferred to A Squadron which was where trade training was undertaken. The last stage was to join the 'Passing Out' Troop, a graduating class of young men ready for full army duty. The JLR RAC Headquarters

Dorian Llewellyn being presented with the trophy for best Junior Leader passing out to the Royal Tank Regiment in 1961 by Field Marshal Sir Bernard Montgomery. (*Dorian Llewellyn*)

Squadron was manned by regular RAC soldiers and civilian instructors required to keep the regiment running.'

These boy soldiers trained in the three RAC trades as part of their education. The emphasis of the programme throughout its forty-one year history was on leadership skills, education, sport, and adventure training. John Webster of the 3rd Carabiniers and Royal Scots Dragoon Guards recalled this important introduction to his army career:

'I passed off with driver, gunner and radio operator trades, during which time we were able to select our regiment of choice to join, though with no guarantee of acceptance. The instructors at the JLR would, if they thought you were any good, try to persuade you to join their regiment. I was a boxer and so the 15th/19th Hussars were after me. I also completed my Parachute Course, and so when I joined the 3rd Carabiniers in Detmold

Richard Allen wearing the 9th/12th Lancers uniform (lance and all), still badged to the JLR as a Lance Orderly prior to passing out in 1969. (Richard Allen)

The 1966 passing out parade, with the uniforms of three different cavalry regiments visible. David Allen, Richard's elder brother, is in the middle. The Allens were a family with a military heritage who had returned from Africa to the UK in the early 1960s. All three sons passed through the Junior Leaders Regiment and served in the Royal Armoured Corps. (*Richard Allen*)

some four months after leaving the JLR, complete with my trades and Parachute Wings, I became the focus of much attention, not all of it welcome! My joining up was the first step of a career that lasted for a total of twenty-five years, badged first to the 3rd Carabiniers and then on amalgamation, to the new regiment, the SCOTS DG.'

The process of entering the Royal Armoured Corps was simple for a regular volunteer. If the candidate had any experience in the Territorial Army or the cadet force he might know much of the expected form already. Often the reasons for volunteering were plain enough. Unemployment was a problem at various times through the entire Cold War. Sometimes the main motive for joining the army was the inability of young men to find the work for which they had apprenticed, or because they saw the army as a means of gaining a trade. Patriotism as another motive could never be ruled out in a land where everyone had a father, uncle, or possibly an older brother who had fought in the Second World War.[17]

After 1960 the Royal Armoured Corps like the rest of the British Army became a volunteer force. It returned to some of the recruiting methods of yore (as well as new ones) to fill its ranks. The familiar image of the recruiting sergeant comes to mind, but the Junior Leaders Regiment RAC, and the KAPE tour also assumed a greater importance attracting recruits after National Service ended. The KAPE (Keeping the Army in the Public Eye) tour in particular was something that veterans tend to remember fondly. A recruiting initiative since the mid-1950s, KAPE tours were put on by regiments in their home recruiting area with the cooperation of the local Territorial Army affiliated regiment. The KAPE tour was highly esteemed because it offered a young trooper a fine opportunity to look his smartest

The 4th/7th Royal Dragoon Guards on a KAPE tour in the early 1970s. The KAPE tour, especially in the early 1960s, was an assignment few regretted. It is unknown how many recruits were attracted in this manner but the tours were always coordinated with the local Territorial Army unit and took place in the regiment's home recruiting area. (*Rob Griffin*)

for the public (and of course for the local ladies), and also because the Territorials were always happy to fete their regular colleagues in the drill hall after duty hours. KAPE tours included some armoured vehicles to show the public, and were generally conducted in a regiment's local recruiting area. Transporting an Antar laden with a Centurion or Chieftain to some of the more remote locations for these public relations events could prove an adventure in itself.

Chapter 3

The Regiment

Throughout the Royal Armoured Corps, as in the infantry, the regiment came first in the hearts of its officers and men. This caused many an outsider to observe that a sense of unity was decidedly lacking in the corps.

> '... the members of the regiments invariably put the RAC last in their list of loyalties, seeing it only as an agency to carry out those complex functions which were beyond regimental means.'[18]

In the 3rd Hussars, as in any cavalry regiment, the traditions of previous centuries were maintained as a great source of pride. Here the Hussars silver kettle drums lead the regimental parade in Iserlohn in 1955. (*Peter Smith*)

John K. Webster of the Royal Scots Dragoon Guards receiving the Good Conduct Medal in ceremonial dress – note the caps and cross belts which differed between cavalry regiments. An army boxing champion, John Webster was posted to the 3rd Carabiniers from the Junior Leaders Regiment, made corporal and sergeant in the following years, and went on to serve in the SCOTS DG upon amalgamation in 1971. (*John K. Webster*)

A remarkable feature that still differentiates the British Army from others is its close attachment to ancient traditions. The Royal Armoured Corps, incorporating the Cavalry and the Household Cavalry (as well as the younger Royal Tank Regiment), keeps some traditions dating back four hundred years. These include the enduring attachment to old customs and ranks found in the cavalry of the line and in the Household Cavalry.

In the Royal Tank Regiment and in the cavalry, life was based around the squadron within the regiment. The Royal Tank Regiment's component regiments called themselves battalions until 1947. The RTR had already adopted the cavalry rank of trooper when the RAC was formed on the eve of the Second World War. Within the sabre squadrons, Squadron Headquarters was home to the Squadron Sergeant Major, holding the rank of WO2 (Warrant Officer 2nd Class). Warrant Officers held their warrant from the secretary of state, set out on an impressive document received on appointment (and which was always a splendid memento to keep on retirement). The badge of the warrant officer was a simple crown on the lower sleeve, (senior warrant officers also wear the crown with laurel leaves surrounding it). This distinguished them from other senior warrant officers (WO1) with appointments such as the Regimental Quartermaster Sergeant Major who would be based in HQ Squadron. The SQMS (Squadron Quarter Master Sergeant) ran the squadron stores with a small staff of other ranks. The most senior non-commissioned officer in the regiment, respected by all and feared by some, was the Regimental Sergeant Major.

The pinnacle of a non-commissioned officer's career was to reach the rank of RSM, especially in the days before officers were promoted from the ranks. Warrant Officer (Class 1) John K. Webster is seen here appointed as the Regimental Sergeant Major of the Royal Scots Dragoon Guards in the mid-1980s. The RSM held a crucial role in the administration and discipline in any regiment. The RSM was also an important keeper of regimental traditions, the symbolism of which can be sensed from the mass of regimental artifacts and honours won by the 3rd Carabiniers and Scots Greys seen in the background. (John K. Webster)

The B Squadron 3rd RTR group portrait taken in 1983. The Royal Tank Regiment had its own traditions despite its relative youth: the ash plant stick carried by its officers, its black overalls and berets and the neck scarves particular to each of the old RTC battalions. (*Dick Taylor*)

Within the armoured squadron, troops were organised under the close watch of a hierarchy of non-commissioned officers. The troop leader (either a lieutenant or a second-lieutenant), troop sergeant, and the troop corporal ran the troop in combat and in day to day duties. A second corporal was usually assigned to a four tank troop. Barring a lone lance corporal, the rest of the troop was made up of troopers. The notorious turnover rate of young officers in armoured regiments sometimes caused troops to be run by staff sergeants. Thus appointed, the staff sergeant was known as a Troop Sergeant Major and was addressed by the other ranks as Staff and by the officers as Sergeant Major.

Anomalies of rank existed with cavalry regiments that did not wear a single chevron rank for lance corporal. They wore a corporal's chevrons for a lance corporal and, for a full corporal, a crown was worn above the chevrons. Regimental bands also caused confusion to the unwary with some of their ranks wearing four chevrons inverted. The lack of rank of sergeant in the Household Cavalry Regiment was always a surprise to outsiders. Part of the intricate Household Cavalry rank system grew from the Life Guards and Royal Horse Guards not having commissioned officers before the middle of the 18th Century.

The Royal Armoured Corps was a part of the British Army where officers worked in very close proximity to their men, as in a tank crew environment the common experience transcends the barriers of rank. This proved as true in the cavalry as it did in the Royal Tank Regiment. The Royal Armoured Corps kept some regimental traditions which brought officers closer to their men. The traditional Christmas dinner arrangement in the 16th/5th Lancers is a fine example also practised elsewhere in the corps:

'At Christmas we had a break for Christmas Day and Boxing Day. Imagine my surprise on my first Christmas morning in the 16th/5th Lancers (in 1959) to be woken by the B Squadron troop sergeants, each with a mess tea bucket filled with either tea or coffee. In their pockets were a bottle each of whisky and rum. You just dug out your pint mug and had it filled with half and half of your choice. Christmas dinner was a blast: we all sat down in a prepared dining hall to be served dinner by the officers, with the regimental band playing on the stage at the end of the hall. Then would come the sketches (that no one was supposed to know about), which took the mickey out of everyone from the colonel down, but all in good taste!'

Harry Wood, 16th/5th Lancers

Despite the teamwork inherent in tank operation and within each squadron, an armoured vehicle was no democracy, and officers (no matter how junior) maintained their station separate and distinct from the other ranks. An officer had a batman or soldier servant, messed apart from the men and usually drank among his fellow officers. In the 1950s and early 1960s officers entered the army by a very different route than the men they commanded, and lived a different military life (though with its own hardships). Lieutenant Frederic Peall of the 3rd Carabiniers recalled the process of becoming an officer in the 1960s.

'The three year short service commission involved six months training at Mons Officer Cadet School, and then two and a half years of service. Regular officers spent three years at the Royal Military Academy Sandhurst, then called the Army University, prior to being commissioned. Apart from academic qualifications, entry was by passing the Regular Commissions Board in Wiltshire. This was three days of tests, both written and practical.

A full squadron arrayed for inspection. This is B Squadron, 5th Royal Inniskilling Dragoon Guards in 1963 operating as a detached squadron at the School of Infantry, Warminster. The markings are for an unbrigaded armoured regiment, 3rd Infantry Division. The squadron deployed sixteen battle tanks, which would include four sabre troops of three tanks, and four tanks at squadron headquarters (one of which was normally fitted as a bulldozer and traditionally commanded by the squadron second in command). The squadron headquarters group is seen behind the line of battle tanks, with the LAD halftrack, a Centurion ARV and a Humber Pig armoured ambulance. Behind these are the squadron commander's Land Rover, the liaison Ferret Mk.1, and the squadron echelon. The lorry served for administration. Most BAOR regiments included a Heavy Troop of three Conquerors in each squadron but this could vary according to manpower and equipment availability. (*Noel McLeery*)

The reconnaissance troop was vital to any armoured regiment and for the period up to the mid-1950s normally consisted of M24 or Cromwell tanks. After 1955 or so these were replaced by the wheeled two man Ferret Mk.2. Here a Ferret Mk.2 of the 3rd Carabiniers reconnaissance troop is seen on the Soltau training area in 1966. (J.K. Webster)

Having passed the RCB, one was enrolled at Sandhurst. There were two entries per year of about two hundred and fifty cadets, so a thousand candidates were in Sandhurst's programme at any one time. Towards the end of the second year one had to get selected for a regiment. I chose the Royal Armoured Corps and was asked for an interview by the colonel of 3rd Carabiniers, Prince of Wales's Dragoon Guards.'

The armoured regiment was commanded by a lieutenant-colonel with a major as second in command and a captain as the adjutant. These officers were the key players in regimental headquarters, but there would also be the regimental signals officer, the gunnery officer, the

The regiment depended on its echelon for all the necessities of life and not just ammunition and fuel. Basic transport tasks were accomplished with the humble four ton lorry like this 1967 photograph of a Bedford of the 9th/12th Lancers. (*Brian Clarke*)

quartermaster, the medical officer, the padre and the other heads of departments, with ranks ranging from major to lieutenant. Depending on conditions, the armoured regiment had three or four sabre squadrons. All these would be commanded by a major, with a captain as second in command. Sometimes the squadron might have had a second captain who would fill the post of battle captain – although only when a regiment was on operations.

Both Montgomery and Field Marshal Slim saw the tradition-bound mentality in some parts of the cavalry's officer corps in the later 1940s as an impediment to the RAC's future. It is impossible to exclude the prejudices of wartime officers (based on perceived failings of the RAC during the early stages of the war) on the post-war treatment of the corps, but many of the criticisms were valid. Uniting the corps was a daunting task in an institution as tradition-bound as the British Army and took decades to fulfil.

In 1947 the RAC had seen early efforts to create a single officers list combining all the cavalry and Royal Tank Regiment's officers fail. The cavalry's long standing traditions and its substantial influence in the army was the problem. Even in the early 1960s the cavalry, like the Guards in the infantry, maintained their old traditions and remained more exclusive than the RTR. Nonetheless, whatever their regiment, officers took their jobs very seriously and professionalism was the hallmark of all RAC regiments. Cavalry was not synonymous with anachronism, but rather with tradition.[19]

In the early part of the Cold War old habits died hard, and the horse was not quite forgotten. Frederic Peall remembers his interview that preceded acceptance into the 3rd Carabiniers:

A 2nd RTR Stalwart Mk.1 loaded with a Ferret Mk.1 in the mid-1960s. A close relative of the Saracen and Saladin, the Alvis Stalwart was a 6x6 all-terrain amphibious load carrier that served until the end of the Cold War. It allowed the regimental echelon a far greater cross country capability. (*Dorian Llewellyn*)

Battlefield logistics capabilities (like refueling or moving up ammunition) were expanded when the amphibious Alvis Stalwart was introduced. The Stalwart Mk.2 had larger windows than the Mk.1, but both employed petrol engines and demanded a complex maintenance regime. (*Brian Clarke*)

Two FV434s lifting a Centurion bulldozer blade for fitting to a Centurion in 1967. The second in command of each armoured squadron normally drove the squadron bulldozer tank. (*Brian Clarke*)

This Centurion bulldozer was a bit of a surprise to the 4th/7th RDG when they took over in Tidworth in the early 1970s. It was unfamiliar and the regiment had already converted to Chieftains but, in the best traditions, it was named *Anti-Arab* after squadron letters. This was all very funny until a military delegation from one of the Arab nations arrived. Without time to paint it out subtle hiding was achieved to prevent any diplomatic incidents. (*R. Griffin*)

A 3rd RTR Scorpion rumbles past the saluting base at the 1985 Standard Parade. The Scorpion was the successor to the little Ferret and offered a far more powerful weapon to the reconnaissance troop in the early 1970s. (*Dick Taylor*)

'I met the colonel at the Cavalry Club, in Piccadilly. The only thing I remember him asking was if I could ride; and he seemed satisfied with the answer, because I was accepted. Having passed out as an infantryman it was then necessary to attend the Royal Armoured Corps Centre at Bovington to learn all about an armoured regiment. A month on D&M, then communications and finally I moved on to Lulworth for gunnery, and tactics. Then it was off to Germany to join my regiment as a Troop Leader.'

Younger officers (second-lieutenants and lieutenants) generally served in two year rotations as troop commanders before promotion. Once an officer made captain, progression became a matter of personal merit, the candidate's perceived potential and the available opportunities (which often arose in a different regiment). Longer serving lieutenants might find themselves commanding one of the HQ Squadron 'departments' and captains might find themselves seconded to brigade level appointments. Since the 1980s it has become more common for enlisted men to be commissioned (at first in roles like regimental quartermaster, but eventually in all roles of regimental command). This trend came as a result in the drop in officer candidates in the late 1970s and early 1980s. Many of these promotions came from experienced NCOs who had been JLR boys. Officers could occasionally attend courses at allied armour schools like those at Munster, Saumur or Fort Knox, and sometimes also served in allied regiments on attachment – more commonly in other Commonwealth armies but also in exchange programmes with other NATO armies. Conversely, officers from allied armies occasionally served in British armoured regiments – most often from the Australian, Canadian or American armies.

A Ferret Mk.2 of the 3rd Carabiniers' reconnaissance troop in 1966. Once the Scorpion arrived at the dawn of the 1970s, the Ferret Mk.2 continued in use outside of BAOR in Northern Ireland, Cyprus and in many other stations. (*Tom Coates*)

Part of the reserve ready to reinforce BAOR or to defend Britain, a regiment was normally stationed at Tidworth throughout the Cold War. Between 1982 and 1984 the 4th RTR took on the role of UK Armoured Regiment/ Warminster Demonstration Squadron. A Squadron was detached to the School of Infantry at Warminster and the rest of the regiment was based at Bhurtpore Barracks, Tidworth. This photo was taken on the 4th RTR tank park and shows a Chieftain undergoing maintenance. (*Keith Paget*)

The Chieftain in due course took on the duties of the squadron second in command's dozer tank. Here we can see *Dolly*, of the 4th RTR at Tidworth in 1984. The red square worn on the side plates was a temporary exercise marking. (*Keith Paget*)

The Ferret Mk.1 long outlived the Mk.2 in the armoured regiments and even served in the 1991 Gulf War. One of the 4th RTR's Mk.1s is seen here with a FV438 in one of the tank hangars at Tidworth in 1984. The Chinese eyes painted on the 4th RTR's tanks first appeared on the Mk.IVs of D Battalion, Royal Tank Corps in the First World War and were worn on all of the 4th RTR's AFVs. (*Keith Pag*et)

A lieutenant of the 1st The Queen's Dragoon Guards on exercise following amalgamation in 1959. Map in hand, binoculars around his neck and standing before two Daimler Armoured Car Mk.2s modernized with smoke dischargers, he typifies a troop leader in the early Cold War period. (*Jumbo Harrison*)

An armoured regiment trained according to the needs of the army and to its assigned schedule. Here a 5th Inniskilling Dragoon Guards Chieftain crawls onto an Antar transporter for the slow drive to a training area in the early 1980s. (*Home Headquarters RDG*)

The RAC's regiments held annual competitions to achieve the highest standards, and to ensure that all strove for excellence. In the 5th Inniskilling Dragoon Guards the Ansell Cup was the annual prize for the best troop in the regiment. This photo of 1st Troop, C Squadron, was taken soon after the 1972 cup presentation by the 5th Inniskilling Dragoon Guards' Regimental Colonel, Sir Michael Ansell. Gunnery, fitness, tactical performance and even aircraft and AFV recognition could be added to training as the commanding officer considered necessary to improve standards. Similar initiatives (always distinct to the character of each regiment) existed throughout the RAC. (*Noel McCleery*)

Tank crews of Headquarters Troop, C Squadron, 5th Inniskilling Dragoon Guards with the Squadron Sergeant Major in 1983. The squadron commander, front row centre, was Major (later Brigadier) Johnny Torrens-Spence with, to his right, the squadron second in command Captain Noel McCleery. These two officers went on to regimental command and regimental second in command respectively. (*Home Headquarters RDG*)

Chapter Four

Korea

The eruption of war in Korea in late 1950 was a rude awakening to the army and to the Royal Armoured Corps. The first armoured detachment was sent to Korea in November 1950. A testament to the depth to which the RAC's stock had sunk was that only sixteen Churchill Mk.VII Crocodiles of the 7th RTR could be raised immediately without weakening BAOR, or the forces in the Middle East. The 7th RTR had returned from India to languish understrength and dispersed, having had a full squadron disbanded. As the RAC's specialised armour regiment it had one squadron of amphibious tanks based at Gosport, and another squadron in Norfolk.

The Churchill Crocodiles of C Squadron, 7th Royal Tank Regiment, were the first tanks to land in Korea in support of 29 Infantry Brigade Group with the leading troop travelling north to Pyongyang on 28 November 1950. At the unfortunately named Battle of Happy Valley, they fought a gallant action together with the Cromwell tanks of Cooper Force on 3 January 1951. (*Private Collection*)

In the bitter winter of 1950–51 the flame throwing equipment was unusable due to the problems finding the right mix of the flame fuel in the appalling cold (with temperatures as low as –47°F) and charging the US sourced nitrogen propellant bottles. Furthermore the trailers were such a serious encumbrance during the retreat southwards along the narrow, icy roads that the majority were backloaded on 12 January 1951. Thereafter the Churchills acted as standard gun tanks except for one troop which retained Crocodiles. All the Churchills were named after the seventh letter of the alphabet such as *George* and *Genie*. Here, a Churchill Mark VII and a Churchill Crocodile pass through the outskirts of the South Korean capital of Seoul on the way to Yongdongpo where the squadron was tasked with protecting the airfield on Seoul Island in April 1951. (Private Collection)

Its equipment was all of 1944 vintage and its manpower shortage caused a crisis getting a full squadron on a war footing and shipped off to Korea. C Squadron was ultimately scraped together from all the professional soldiers in the regiment, as the best that could be managed. The regiment nearest to Korea, 3rd RTR in Hong Kong, could not be sent because of the threat posed by the communist Chinese. Nobody was equipped or ready for the brutal cold of a Korean winter.

The 7th RTR squadron arrived first to support the 29th Infantry Brigade in Korea. They were soon joined by the 8th Hussars, with new Centurion Mk.3s. The 8th Hussars had brought their reconnaissance troop equipped with Cromwell tanks, and when the Centurions were temporarily withdrawn during the sudden retreat of the UN forces in late November 1950, the few old Churchills and Cromwells were temporarily the only British tanks in the front line. The small force of Cromwells (fighting as Cooper Force, with meagre numbers bolstered by some artillery observation post tanks armed only with machine guns) and the 7th RTR squadron were engaged in heavy fighting supporting separate brigades. The Churchills

Cooper Force consisted of the combined Cromwells of the 8th KRIH reconnaissance troop, and of the 29th Infantry Brigade's artillery regiment (the 45th Field Regiment, Royal Artillery, whose tanks included some artillery observation post vehicles with dummy guns, like the vehicle seen here). Tasked, under the command of Captain Astley-Cooper, with covering the Royal Ulster Rifles withdrawal only five Hussars and nine artillerymen escaped out of the force of sixty-five on the night of 3 January 1951. (*Crown Copyright*)

were put to good use driving back enemy infantry attacks, but the communist forces were better organised than anyone in Washington and London realised. While covering the withdrawal of the 29th Brigade, Cooper Force was encircled and wiped out in one of the tragic episodes in the UN retreat. This was a bloody nose for the UN, and a tragedy for the 8th Hussars which caused bitter criticism of the command of the UN forces by the commanding officer of the Hussars in his correspondence with the Director Royal Armoured Corps. The Churchills of the 7th RTR stayed in theatre until October 1951 and had a successful campaign.[20]

The 8th Hussars had also been strengthened with men drafted in from all over the RAC, but could not be committed as a full regiment until February 1951. The stabilization of the UN position in the following weeks allowed the 8th Hussars to establish themselves, to gain cohesion and to quickly demonstrate their capabilities in the harsh Korean winter. The disaster of Cooper Force was never given the publicity it deserved and was never repeated. Perhaps the greatest loss of life sustained by the Royal Armoured Corps in one action since 1945, it would have caused an outcry at home had it not been hushed up. It was a firm reminder of the perils of fighting under foreign command and of the risks associated with unpreparedness. Of the sixty-five men in the Cooper Force, fifty-one were killed and missing.

In 1950 the 8th Kings Royal Irish Hussars deployed hurriedly to Korea including a large number of reservists to make up their war establishment. This photo was taken of the Centurion Mk.3 *Colombo* on the Han River on 20 December 1950. *Colombo* is already equipped with the second pattern cast turret built from 1950 onwards without a rear access door. The two tankers are Troopers Alex Veysey of Edmonton, London and Charles Smith (the driver) of Matlock, Derbyshire. (*NARA with thanks to Steve Zaloga*)

All fourteen Cromwells from the two regiments involved (the 8th Hussars and 45th Field Regiment Royal Artillery) were also lost. These risks were inherent in the existing state of the RAC in 1950. The Royal Armoured Corps handled the continuing deployment to Korea in the next two years effectively, but there was always a need to build up the armoured regiment supporting the Commonwealth Division with detached personnel from the entire corps.

The third Battle of the Hook, which raged during the night of May 28–29 1953 after a week-long artillery bombardment, gives a good idea of the type of war the regiments fought in Korea. C Squadron, 1st Royal Tank Regiment supported the 29th Infantry Brigade through the action, mainly alongside the 1st Battalion, Duke of Wellington's Regiment. During a whole night fighting as mobile direct fire artillery, the squadron's fourteen Centurions fired over five hundred 20-pounder rounds, fourteen thousand rounds of 7.92mm Besa and five thousand rounds of .30 Browning. Several tanks took direct hits but no losses were suffered – a testament to the durability of the Centurion. The entire support group assigned to C Squadron, including fitters and cooks, helped to keep the tanks stocked with ammunition and fuel.[21]

Colombo wears the white star carried by all UN Forces in Korea as a recognition sign. In a large coalition, this reduced the risk of fratricidal incidents. By 29 December the Centurions were being pulled back to avoid encirclement by a massive Chinese supported North Korean offensive; this led to the tragedy of Cooper Force. (*NARA with thanks to Steve Zaloga*)

Colombo with a Centaur Bulldozer near the Han River in Korea, 20 December 1950. Writing in his early days in Korea to the Director Royal Armoured Corps, the commanding officer of the 8th Kings Royal Irish Hussars doubted the suitability of the Centurion to the Korean terrain due to its size and weight. His doubts were soon dispelled and, in the next two years, the Centurion proved itself perhaps the best tank in service anywhere. (*NARA with thanks to Steve Zaloga*)

Warfare in Korea was reminiscent of the war in Italy and even in places of the First World War. It was a war of infantry support missions and artillery engagements for the tanks. It was an eye opener to the complacency of the government's misguided post-war army manpower policy.[22] A full regiment was kept in Korea for the remainder of the conflict, supported by a Canadian squadron in Sherman tanks. The Centurions never engaged enemy tanks (other than blowing up a captured Cromwell) but the troopers honed their skills in their new tank. By the end of the war, not only had the 7th RTR, the 8th Hussars, the 5th Inniskilling Dragoon Guards, the 1st RTR and the 5th RTR served in the Commonwealth Division, but officers and men from every regiment in the corps had swelled their ranks.

Tank crews of No.12 Troop C Squadron, 6th RTR in Libya in 1956. Some of the tanks still carry the black turret bands applied for Operation Musketeer. The tank on the right is named *Lazy Jane*. (*Pete Dobson*)

Chapter Five

The 1950s

The direct result of communist aggression in Asia was the enlargement of BAOR as the RAC's key strategic commitment. The activation of the 1st British Corps as the heart of the British Army of the Rhine on 18th June 1951 required the reactivation of the 6th, 7th and 11th Armoured Divisions. The process had already begun in 1950 and was completed by 1952. The army was as large as the peacetime economy could bear, and 1st British Corps was intended

An inspection of a 2nd Royal Tank Regiment Centurion in the early 1950s. Throughout that decade the arm of service and formation insignia was carried on the front and rear of each tank although, depending on the unit, these could be painted on the glacis plate, the front mudguards, or on the upper corners of the lower front plate. (*MP Robinson collection*)

Royal Armoured Corps Order of Battle, 1952

Regiment	Garrison	Formation (Bde, Div, Corps)
The Life Guards	Wolfenbuttel	11th Armoured Division
The Royal Horse Guards	Windsor	3rd Division UK
1st The Kings's Dragoon Guards	Hamburg/Rahlstedt	6th Armoured Division
2nd Dragoon Guards (Queen's Bays)	Fallingbostel	7th Armoured Bde/7AD
3rd Carabiniers (Prince of Wales's Dragoon Guards)	Osnabruck	20th Armoured Bde/6AD
4th/7th Royal Dragoon Guards	Libya	25th Armoured Brigade
5th Royal Inniskilling Dragoon Guards	Korea	Commonwealth Division
The Royal Dragoons (1st Dragoons)	Egypt	10th Armoured Division MELF
The Royal Scots Greys (2nd Dragoons)	Aldershot	3rd Division UK
3rd (The Kings Own) Hussars	Bielefeld	11th Armoured Division
4th Queen's Own Hussars	Tidworth	3rd Division UK
7th Queen's Own Hussars	Fallingbostel	7th Armoured Division
8th King's Royal Irish Hussars	Luneberg	7th Armoured Bde/7AD
9th Queen's Royal Lancers	Detmold	33rd Armoured Bde/11AD
12th (Prince of Wales) Royal Lancers	Malaya	British Forces Far East
16th/5th Lancers	Libya	25th Armoured Brigade
17th/21st Lancers	Munster	20 Armoured Bde/6AD
10th Royal Hussars (Prince of Wales's Own)	Iserlohn	2nd Infantry Division
11th Hussars (Prince Albert's Own)	Wesendorf	7th Armoured Division
13th/18th Royal Hussars (Queen Mary's Own)	Malaya	British Forces Far East
14th/20th Kings Hussars	Libya	25th Armoured Brigade
15/19th The King's Royal Hussars	Neumunster	I Br Corps
1st Royal Tank Regiment	Detmold	33rd Armoured Bde/11AD
2nd Royal Tank Regiment	Munster	20 Armoured Bde/6AD
3rd Royal Tank Regiment	Tidworth	3rd Division UK
4th Royal Tank Regiment	Egypt	25th Armoured Brigade
5th Royal Tank Regiment	Hohne	7th Armoured Bde/7AD
6th Royal Tank Regiment	Munster	20 Armoured Bde/6AD
7th Royal Tank Regiment	Hong Kong	40th Infantry Division
8th Royal Tank Regiment	Detmold	33rd Armoured Bde/11AD
1st Independent Squadron Royal Tank Regiment	West Berlin	British Troops Berlin
BAOR Units		

to include four armoured divisions, and four infantry divisions. This massive force was never raised, but BAOR was brought up to a four division corps by the end of 1952.[23]

In 1950 the 11th Armoured Division was reborn in West Germany. The re-equipment of the new division and of the 6th Armoured Division in Britain for deployment to West Germany in 1951 took over a year. Each of the new armoured divisions was armed with Centurions. In 1951 the 1st (Berlin) Independent Squadron RTR was formed, institutionalising an RAC presence (and in the later part of the Cold War, a *permanent* presence) in West Berlin. A belated answer to the Berlin crisis three years earlier, this squadron changed in name several times over the next fifteen years, being disbanded in the reduction of the army in 1957 but reappearing again in the early 1960s. The NATO Northern Army Group (NORTHAG) was formed in late November 1952, with BAOR as a central component defending an area from Hamburg to Kassel. Very soon NORTHAG took on a multinational character with German, Dutch, Belgian, French and American formations alongside the British. In the early 1950s BAOR also received a Canadian mechanised infantry brigade armed with British and American equipment, and based around Soest (until its 1970 move to CENTAG).

Combat experience accumulated on the Centurion led to many detail improvements and the re-evaluation of some tactical and equipment related issues for the armoured units in BAOR. The Korean War pushed the development of the Heavy Gun Tank for BAOR's armoured regiments. The top brass of the British Army greatly feared Soviet heavy tank designs like the Iosif Stalin 3, and they demanded a 120mm gunned tank to provide added firepower to Centurion regiments. Following the FV201 project's cancellation, FVRDE's

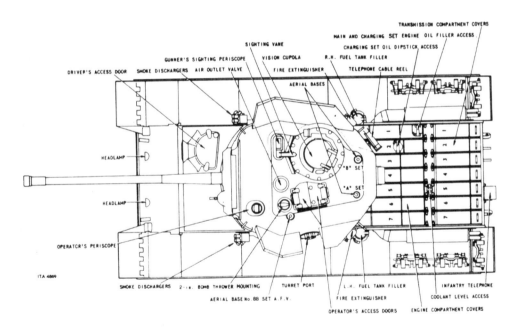

Fig.1 Plan view of vehicle

The Caernarvon was tested by the 14th/20th Hussars amongst others and the experience of operating such a large tank was used to prepare the rest of the Royal Armoured Corps for the Conqueror. The layout of the hull is seen here. The Tank Museum's Conqueror started life as a Caernarvon and was rebuilt to Conqueror standard at the end of the production run. (*Crown Copyright*)

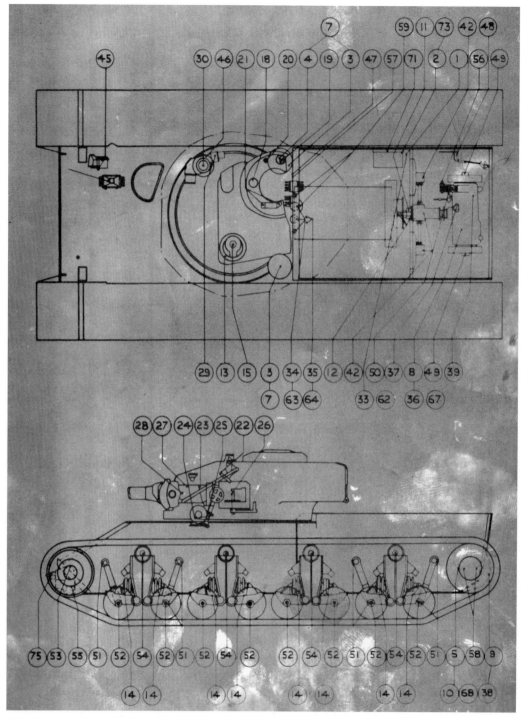

The dimensions of the Caernarvon were impressive in most respects – other than the turret which was typical of late production Mk.3 or Mk.5 Centurion (*Crown Copyright*)

designers also realised that a 120mm gun was required. The only suitable 120mm weapon was American and time was not available to develop a British alternative. If bought off the shelf, the American gun could not fire the types of ammunition favoured by the British. FVRDE indicated that given the need to develop a complete turret, a fire control system and ammunition, production before January 1954 would be impossible. The use of the FV201 hull as the basis for the Heavy Gun Tank made sense because the turret ring size required would fit. The decision was taken to proceed under the new specification FV214 and the resulting vehicle was later named Conqueror.

The Conqueror arrived in 1955 with excellent firepower and armour, powered by a fuel injected version of the same Meteor used in the Centurion. The Conqueror's design was unique for including a separate Fire Control Turret with a range finder (known as the FCT) for the commander. The commander's role was to locate and range each target, and then hand the engagement over to the gunner, while he searched for the next target. This was a new concept in British gunnery but one that later became known as the 'hunter killer system'. It was never a popular tank to serve on: its specialist role was complex and it was never particularly reliable.[24]

The Conqueror presented a challenge to its crews and was regarded with a mixture of awe and trepidation upon its arrival in the armoured regiments. No new tactical doctrine accompanied it, and to some officers it represented a nuisance more than anything else. In the 1956 journal of the 3rd Hussars, the first Conquerors were described as 'The Brutes' because

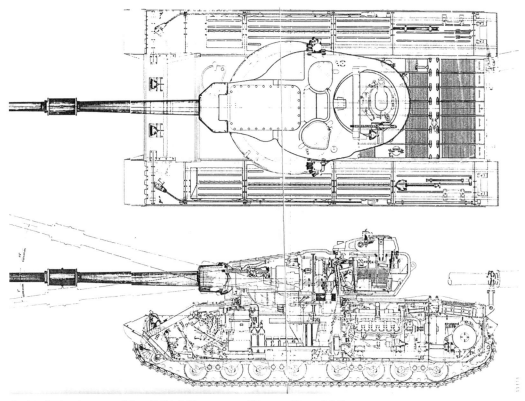

A detailed cut away of the FV214 Conqueror. (Crown Copyright)

of their massive presence. The 3rd Hussars journal for 1957 recounts a C Squadron Conqueror nicknamed *Her Majesty's Battleship Carefree*, and her first turn on the ranges. Accounts in the journals of the 3rd Carabiniers and of the 16th/5th Lancers in the following few years recount that mishaps and mechanical fragility were common. Nocturnal exercises seem to have been especially dangerous, and there were accidents of all types, including collisions. The Heavy Gun Tank was a weapon that needed a committed crew and mastery of its sophisticated fire control system needed regular use. The Centurion's capacity to fire two or three rounds within split seconds was impossible on a Conqueror with its two piece ammunition.[25]

Nearly three thousand Centurions (and over one hundred and fifty five Conquerors) had been delivered by 1956, and British armaments sold in quantities that were never again equalled. The Centurion was a mature design which was already appreciated by the Royal Armoured Corps at all levels. In the 1950s the armoured regiments dealt with many changes as new weapons became available but the tactics and structure of the armoured brigades remained constant (even with the arrival of the Conqueror). In some cases the needs of the moment pushed weapons programmes ahead, but most changes were incremental. From 1954 FVRDE concentrated on several projects to ensure BAOR's future ability to defeat future Soviet threats. These included the redesign of the Centurion to permit longer range, more powerful armament and better protection. A new 105mm gun based on the 20-pounder was also developed, and emerged in 1959 as the L7. With the very successful Centurion developments lay some failed ventures, including self-propelled guns on the Centurion chassis.

In 1954 the RAC disbanded the 65th, 66th, 67th and 68th Training Regiments to retain regular regiments. Thereafter the role of RAC Training Regiment was assigned in two year rotations at Catterick Camp. The Training Regiment was tasked with increasing duties as the

Carefree, a Conqueror Mk.1 of the 3rd Hussars' C Squadron, on the ranges in 1957 as originally seen in the 3rd Hussars magazine. Only fifteen FV214 Conqueror Mk.1s were built and the 3rd Hussars received several – of which the first arrived in mid-1955. (Peter Smith)

Two troopers standing before a Conqueror Mk.1 of the 3rd Hussars in Iserlohn. The black 59 on the yellow and red diagonally divided square was one of several markings used to denote an unbrigaded armoured regiment while the crossed key emblem is that of the 2nd Infantry Division. This Conqueror, as an aside, is suspected to be the one preserved at *Le Musée des Blindées* at Saumur. (*Peter Smith*)

A 3rd Hussars Conqueror Mk.1 from B Squadron photographed on the Iserlohn tank park in 1956. *The Brutes* (as the 3rd Hussars Conquerors were called) were grouped in a heavy troop in each squadron with three Conquerors. This one is named *Bonzo*. Note how the smoke discharger covers carry the last two digits of the registration number. (*Peter Smith*)

A 3rd Hussars A Squadron Conqueror Mk.1 named *Advent* and flying the skull and crossbones flag. (*Peter Smith*)

A Conqueror Mk.2 of an unknown regiment, probably in West Germany. The background includes a Centurion and the trackless hull of a wartime Ram Kangaroo – a vehicle used in some regiments in the early 1950s as a driver trainer and as an APC. (*MP Robinson Collection*)

Cleaning the barrel of a Conqueror's L1A1 120mm gun in 1956 or 1957. (*Peter Smith*)

1950s progressed to the 1960s and eventually trained troops for both armoured car regiments and armoured regiments. Training was still conducted with recruits passing through three different squadrons. A Squadron conducted the most basic military training, B Squadron education and trades, and C Squadron functioned as a holding squadron to put on the finishing touches.[26]

After 1955 the organization of BAOR began another metamorphosis to balance defending the corps area with the stark fact that the army had grown too large. There were eighty thousand men in West Germany – too many to exist indefinitely on the national budget. The composition of BAOR and the locations of its garrisons underwent substantial changes in 1955–1956 – largely because of the establishment of the new West German *Bundeswehr* which needed its own training areas and bases. As the size of the continental European NATO armies increased after 1956 the size of 1st British Corps decreased. These changes permitted the remaining weapons of the wartime era to be finally retired. The BAOR headquarters moved to Bad Oynhausen in 1956.

In 1956 the aftermath of Operation Musketeer (which became the Suez crisis despite its military success) brought a cold hard dose of reality. The 1st and 6th Royal Tank Regiments participated in the operation and other regiments in Germany (like the 3rd Hussars) were placed on high alert to reinforce them if it became necessary, but they waited in vain and the operation damaged British credibility. The reduction of the 1st British Corps led BAOR towards a brigade-based structure instead of divisions as the basic large formations. The shrinking defence budget was outlined in the 1957 White Paper prepared under the direction

The 3rd Hussars tank park at Iserlohn in the mid-1950s. Vehicle maintenance consumed much time in an average week but the tank park was quieter at weekends when leave was available. (*Peter Smith*)

Sergeant Piotrowski's Centurion Mk.7 of the 3rd Hussars on a battle run on Soltau in 1956. Piotrowski was one of several Polish soldiers who had fought in the Free Polish Army in the Second World War and who went on to serve in the 3rd Hussars. (*Peter Smith*)

Lunch on the Soltau training area with the 3rd Hussars in 1956. Without a visible fire, we can suppose that the victuals might have included items heated up in the Centurion's boiling vessel. (*Peter Smith*)

An A Squadron Centurion Mk.3 or Mk.5 of the 3rd Hussars named *Aggressive* in 1956. The impressive dust cloud indicates dry weather, and a spare road wheel is fixed to the track stowage bracket on the rear of the turret. This was reputedly the regiment's fastest Centurion at the time and was commanded by Sergeant Allen. (*Peter Smith*)

A Squadron, 3rd Hussars tanks on the firing ranges in the mid-1950s. All are fitted with fuel trailers and type A 20-pounder barrels, which would suggest Centurion Mk.3s and Mk.5s. (*Peter Smith*)

An 8th RTR Centurion Mk.8 being recovered in 1956. (*P. Bettany*)

An 8th RTR Centurion Mk.8 being winched out of the mud on the Soltau training ground. (*P. Bettany*)

A 3rd Hussars Conqueror crew in 1955. The Conqueror had a poor record for reliability but, when all systems were functioning, it was an impressive and imposing vehicle. Many of its design principles, such as the hunter-killer fire control system, were ahead of their time and were taken up in modern MBTs. It was faster than the Centurion and wider tracks gave it an improved ability to cross broken terrain. Electronic technology in the 1950s tank fire control system was basic and even the most advanced system worked on mechanical linkages and simple switches. (*Peter Smith*)

Admiral of the 3rd Hussars, having backed over its monowheel trailer during training in West Germany, at some time in the 1955–56 period. (*Peter Smith*)

In dry conditions on the West German training grounds, dust could become a major problem when tanks moved at speed. (*Peter Smith*)

Prepared for wading and marked for Operation Musketeer, this tank is most likely a 1st RTR vehicle photographed on Malta in 1956. One clue is that the arm of service insignia number is 54 instead of the 59 worn by the 6th RTR tanks involved in the Suez landings. (*Crown Copyright*)

A Centurion of the 1st Royal Tank Regiment during wading trials on Malta in 1956. The 1st RTR was to have supported the Suez landings with the 6th Royal Tank Regiment but their timely arrival was delayed due to naval loading priorities. The Suez Centurions were prominently marked with a black band painted around the turret and a large letter H in white on the turret roof – markings also applied to the 1st RTR's tanks in anticipation of the landing. (*Crown Copyright*)

of defence minister Duncan Sandys. National Service was to be abolished in stages, and national defence policy was reoriented (irrevocably) towards Europe. It was a final admission that the empire had disappeared and that the remaining colonies would become independent.[27]

The army tried desperately to minimize the number of historic regiments to be disbanded. In the Royal Armoured Corps the cuts were as harsh as anywhere: the 11th Armoured Division was disbanded after less than seven years of renewed existence and was reformed as the 4th Infantry Division. The famed 7th Armoured Division was renumbered as the 5th Armoured Division, and the 6th Armoured Division amalgamated with the 2nd Infantry Division. Thereafter BAOR was reduced to 64,000 men. The cavalry shrank by three regiments as did the Royal Tank Regiment, in two painful rounds of amalgamations that took place over four years between 1957 and 1961. The Territorial Army's Royal Tank Regiments, and many of the Yeomanry regiments of the cavalry, disappeared entirely as a result of the 1957 White Paper. The 10th Armoured Division in Libya was also disbanded.[28]

The amalgamations affected no less than twelve regular regiments and took place as follows:

The 1st King's Own Dragoon Guards and 2nd Queen's Bays became the 1st Queen's Own Dragoon Guards. The 3rd King's Own Hussars and 7th Queen's Own Hussars became the

The tank crew. Lieutenant Frederic Peall was a troop leader in the 3rd Carabiniers. The tank crew was a team and the members worked for the most part harmoniously on many tasks. Officers remained a breed apart – a necessity that permitted them to command and control hard situations in time of war. (*Frederic Peall*)

Queen's Own Hussars in 1957. The 4th Queen's Own Hussars and 8th King's Royal Irish Hussars became the Queen's Royal Irish Hussars. The 3rd RTR and 6th RTR amalgamated to become the 3rd RTR. The 4th RTR and the 7th RTR amalgamated and became the 4th RTR. The 5th RTR and 8th RTR amalgamated and became the 5th RTR. The 9th and 12th Lancers were the last regiments to be amalgamated as a result of the 1957 White Paper (their union taking place in 1960 at Tidworth). Amalgamations were a painful process which the corps would come to know well. Each of the six "new" regiments found cohesion rapidly despite the shock of change.

The regimental journal of 1958 for the 3rd Hussars recounts amalgamation very stoically, with every indication that it would be a happy union. The 3rd made a special point of saluting the record of their brother hussar regiment.

'The value of the regimental history to the living soldier is the example of achievement through training, discipline, determination, courage and offensive spirit. The 7th and the 3rd Hussars have so often shown these qualities on the battlefields of the past. These are the qualities, which their successors will now need to make The Queen's Own Hussars a great regiment.'[29]

The officers of both regiments did all they could to keep the most important traditions and spirit of each unit. The amalgamation had come as a surprise to the 3rd, whose men first heard the news on the ranges at Hohne: the 7th Hussars heard in transit back to Britain, and the amalgamation occurred at Tidworth in September 1958.

In some regiments the maintenance of common traditions made the process easier to accept. The union eventually went smoothly for the 9th/12th Lancers despite the fact that the 9th were an armoured regiment in BAOR and the 12th Lancers were an armoured reconnaissance regiment fresh from Malaya. Peter Dobson recalled the 1959 amalgamation of the 3rd Royal Tank Regiment with the 6th Royal Tank Regiment then returning from Libya.

'When the 6th Royal Tank Regiment left Homs, Libya in August 1959, a hundred and thirty men were left behind to join the incoming 2nd Royal Tank Regiment. The rest of the regiment moved to Detmold, West Germany. The amalgamation was held on the airstrip at Sennelager on October 31st, 1959. We all wore No.1 dress (our blues) with white gloves. Sir Harold Pyman, who served with both the 6th and the 3rd during the war, took the salute. Despite the rain the whole parade went off perfectly. The windmill on the airstrip was painted green (for the 3rd RTR) and red and yellow (for the 6th RTR) to mark the occasion. The integration of the two regiments went very well as I recall (as you must remember we all wore the same cap badge so we were all 'tankies') even though I was disappointed to lose my red and yellow shoulder flash. We were now officially 'The New 3rd' and we went from strength to strength as a regiment.'

A Centurion Mk.5 of the 4th Guards Armoured Brigade Group onboard a West German landing craft during an exercise in the late 1950s or early 1960s. The tank is likely crewed either by the 5th Royal Inniskilling Dragoon Guards or the 17th/21st Lancers – both of whom served in this brigade in the period. The Guards Brigade's all-seeing eye emblem is visible on the rear plate, along with a Union Jack decal and yellow/red arm of service denoting an armoured regiment attached to an infantry brigade. (*MP Robinson collection*)

In the mid-1950s the British Army adopted the Centurion Mk.7 with many design improvements as a result of service in Korea and West Germany. The vehicles adopted a Deep Bronze Green colour scheme which looked smart for parades but dulled down nicely into a good basic camouflage after a few hours on the training ground – as on the 3rd Carabiniers Mk.7 seen here in the early 1960s. (*Frederic Peall*)

The Centurion Mk.7 and Mk.8 seen here were FVRDE improvements of the basic Centurion that entered service in 1955–1956. These are 3rd Carabiniers tanks seen in 1965. (*Frederic Peall*)

Firing ranges in desert areas were relatively easy to set up due to the sparse population. Here we can see two 6th RTR Centurion Mk.3s in 1956 pausing to look over an unfortunate M5 Stuart target. (*Pete Dobson*)

Chapter Six

1959–1969: The RAC Focused on BAOR

By the 1960s the three main Royal Armoured Corps bases were the Royal Armoured Corps Centre at Bovington Camp, Tidworth in Hampshire and Catterick Camp in Yorkshire. These were the training establishments for the whole Royal Armoured Corps. Gunnery ranges at Lulworth, Castlemartin, Warcop and Kirkudbright were essential satellites. The last National Service conscripts were discharged in 1962–1963. The available strength in BAOR dropped in the late 1950s down to 55,000 men. Brigade groups replaced armoured and infantry divisions

Centurion Armoured Vehicle Launched Bridges, or more simply bridgelayers, appeared in armoured regiment headquarters troops in the late 1960s. Here we can just about make out the bulk of a bridgelayer behind this Centurion ARV Mk.2 of the 9th/12th Lancers on exercise in West Germany. (*Brian Clarke*)

Royal Armoured Corps Order of Battle, June 1962

Regiment 1962 (June)	Garrison	Brigade Group	Division or Formation
The Life Guards	Herford	Corps Armoured Car Regiment	1st British Corps
The Royal Horse Guards	Windsor	Corps Armoured Car Regiment	1st British Corps
1st The Queen's Dragoon Guards (QDG)	Wolfenbuttel	Corps Armoured Car Regiment	1st British Corps
3rd Carabiniers (Prince of Wales's Dragoon Guards)	Tidworth	UK Reconnaissance Regiment	3rd Division
4th/7th Royal Dragoon Guards (4/7RDG)	Catterick	Training Regiment RAC	3rd Division
5th Royal Inniskilling Dragoon Guards (5DG)	Sennelager	4th Guards	4th Guards
The Royal Dragoons (1st Dragoons)	Tidworth	UK Armoured Regiment	3rd Division
The Royal Scots Greys (2nd Dragoons)	Detmold	20th Armoured	1st Division
The Queen's Own Hussars	Munster	6th Infantry	1st Division
The Queen's Royal Irish Hussars	Aden	Armoured Car Regiment	British Forces South Arabia
9th/12th Royal Lancers (Prince of Wales's)	Omagh (NI)	UK Reconnaissance Regiment	3rd Division
16/5th The Queen's Royal Lancers	Osnabruck	12th Infantry	2nd Division
17th/21st Lancers	Aden/Hong Kong	Detached Armoured Regiment	BF S.Arabia, BF Far East
10th Royal Hussars (Prince of Wales's Own)	Paderborn	5th Infantry	4th Division
11th Hussars (Prince Albert's Own)	Tidworth	UK Armoured Regiment	3rd Division
13th/18th Royal Hussars (Queen Mary's Own)	Fallingbostel	7th Armoured	1st Division
14th/20th Kings Hussars	Libya/Hohne	7th Armoured	1st Division
15th/19th The King's Royal Hussars	Munster	Nuclear Escort Armoured Car	1st British Corps
1st Royal Tank Regiment	Hohne	11th Infantry	2nd Division
2nd Royal Tank Regiment	Tripoli	Detached Armoured Regiment	British Forces Middle East
3rd Royal Tank Regiment	Detmold	20th Armoured	1st Division
4th Royal Tank Regiment (less B Sqn)	Lemgo, Celle	Corps APC Regiment	1st British Corps
5th Royal Tank Regiment	Fallingbostel	7th Armoured	1st Division
Parachute Squadron 2nd Royal Tank Regiment	UK	16th Airborne Brigade	UK General Reserve
Special Recce Squadron RAC	Paderborn	1st British Corps	1st British Corps
B Squadron 4th RTR	Berlin	Berlin Field Force	1st British Corps

A whole squadron of Centurions on the ranges at Hohne in 1967. The Centurion was a vehicle for which many crewmen developed lasting affection. We can see the range flags on these tanks of the 9th/12th Lancers, green indicating that the weapons are unloaded. The 9th/12th Lancers at the time were based in Osnabruck, West Germany. (*Brian Clarke*)

Three late model Centurions of the 9th/12th Lancers in 1967 on the Hohne ranges, all armed with the L7 105mm gun. From left to right are a Centurion Mk.13 with infrared searchlight fitted, a Centurion Mk. 6 with the armoured fuel cell bolted to the rear plate (and which was a rebuilt Mk.3 or Mk.5), and a Centurion Mk.12 without its searchlight fitted. Centurion units by 1967 were waiting for the new Chieftain and usually hosted quite a mix of new and rebuilt vehicles. (*Brian Clarke*)

as the basis of the 1st British Corps. This was a preamble to the reorganization of BAOR in the early 1960s, in a bewildering series of changes in the 1st Corps order of battle. In 1960 BAOR comprised eight brigade groups, which would form three divisions in the event of war. These were the 7th and 20th Armoured Brigade Groups, the 4th Canadian Mechanized Brigade, and the 4th Guards, 5th, 6th 11th and 12th Infantry Brigade Groups.[30]

The four Independent Infantry Brigade Groups were each assigned an armoured regiment as part of their brigade structure, allowing each to function as a mechanised brigade with new Saracen APCs. The armoured regiments allocated to the independent infantry brigade groups would expect to serve in detached squadrons or as a concentrated regiment, depending on the tactical situation. For the two armoured brigade groups, the next significant event was the recreation of the 1st Armoured Division headquarters in BAOR in 1960. The formation changes that came fast and furious in the next few years mainly affected the creation of divisional headquarters for use in time of war. As soon as the 5th Armoured Division headquarters was reactivated from the cadre of the 7th Armoured Division headquarters, it was renamed the 1st Armoured Division.

The divisional honours and identities were preserved wherever possible, having been parcelled out to the brigades in the previous two years. The 20th Armoured Brigade had carried the 6th Armoured Division's mailed fist insignia ever since the latter had stood down. The 7th Armoured Brigade carried on the red gerboa insignia made so famous by the 7th Armoured Division. The marking systems of the 1950s also disappeared as the army assumed

A Centurion Mk.8 of A Squadron, call sign 12B, the 3rd Carabiniers broken down on the Salisbury Plain training area in 1960. The engine decks are raised and the crew awaits the LAD detachment. (*Barrie Dady*)

A 3rd Carabiniers Centurion Mk.6 in 1963. The Centurion Mk.6 was the Mk.5 (most of which were upgraded Centurion Mk.3s) rearmed with the potent L7 105mm gun. Many of the Mk.6s also received the long range fuel tank in place of the rotten old monowheel trailer. (*Tom Coates*)

a more sober look for the 1960s.[31] In the following years cost cutting measures by the government brought more reductions which took BAOR below the manpower level required for a corps on wartime footing. In a bewildering set of further reductions and amalgamations, the brigade groups reverted back to being called simple brigades in 1965 (although the four regiment brigades that were adopted in the ensuing few years became known as 'square brigades'). In 1967 the surviving Territorial Army RAC units were reassigned to supply trained replacement AFV crews for the regular RAC regiments and ceased to train as functional regiments.[32]

Somewhat apart from BAOR in West Berlin there was also the Berlin Squadron detached from the Tidworth-based strategic reserve regiment. In the 1960s and early 1970s this consisted of thirteen Centurions, which were later replaced by Chieftains. In the 1960s the Berlin Squadron had some tense moments, but the men settled down to higher level of readiness extremely well. The squadron operated deep in East Germany, and travelling to West Berlin by train was usually the subject of much curiosity.

'Unlike all other BAOR or UK based armoured regiments the Berlin Squadron had to be at almost immediate readiness to move in the event of any International crisis developing between NATO and the Warsaw Pact countries. To that end all of the tanks had to be ready for action within thirty minutes of being alerted, with one troop in a permanent state of readiness and able to leave barracks within ten to fifteen minutes. A second troop was based, on a monthly rotational basis with the other three troops, within the confines of the Berlin Brigade Headquarters immediately adjacent to the Berlin Olympic swimming pool.

In 1961–1963, the 4th RTR was tasked as a 1st British Corps unbrigaded regiment. A and B squadrons served as APC crews equipped with Saracens in the 7th and 20th Armoured Brigades, and C Squadron served in West Berlin. Here we can see the tanks employed by the US, French and British armoured units in West Berlin. The M48 was an American medium roughly comparable to the 4th RTR's Centurion Mk.5s, while the little AMX-13 was a light tank weighing about 14 tons. Note how *Discoverer* has the obligatory Chinese eyes worn by the 4th RTR's tanks since the First World War. (*4th RTR with thanks to Michael Rose*)

The Berlin Squadron was always a special posting. It had its origins in the Berlin Squadron Royal Tank Regiment of the early 1950s but it underwent a metamorphosis of different designations and incarnations before the late 1960s. The 9th/12th Lancers, stationed in Tidworth as the strategic reserve regiment in 1970, supplied the squadron at the same time. (*Richard Allen*)

Preparing for the 1970 Allied Forces Parade, which included British, French and American units stationed in West Berlin.

With the turret traversed the second opening for the 12.7mm ranging gun is visible mounted next to the coaxial machinegun. For simplicity the British Army preferred to use the ranging gun instead of developing an optical rangefinder like some of the other NATO armies. (*Brian Clarke*)

Centurion Mk.12, an adaptation of the Centurion Mk.7 based Centurion Mk.9 with infrared capabilities. The photographer of this series of 9th/12th Lancers Centurions was a REME electronics technician and knew the infrared gear inside and out! Even after it was replaced by the Chieftain, the Centurion continued in service into the 1980s and 1990s with other armies as a gun tank. (*Brian Clarke*)

The 20th Armoured Brigade lined up in review order for the birthday of HM Queen Elisabeth II in 1965. These are Centurions and Conquerors of the 3rd Carabiniers. An early Centurion Mk.10 with L7 105mm gun is visible as are other Centurions as far as the eye can see. (*Barrie Dady*)

The crew of a 9th/12th Lancers Centurion Mk.13 broken down in 1967. In such a situation the whole crew is involved in getting the vehicle ready for the REME LAD detachment. The stoutly built basket fitted to the turret rear held the dismounted infrared projector when it was not fitted to the gun mantlet as well as necessities (such as bedding, ration boxes and even folding chairs) which could be crammed in by an experienced crew for use on exercise. (*Brian Clarke*)

'The high state of readiness ensured that the tanks were all permanently fully loaded with live ammunition and fuel at all times. The only items that were not in situ on the vehicles were the Browning .50″ ranging gun, two Browning .30″ machine guns and the crews' personal weapons. These would be issued within minutes of an alarm being raised. This gave us an additional workload because each vehicle's full complement of ammunition had to be unloaded, counted and inspected a minimum of once per month. The fact that these tanks were fully operational didn't seem to have any effect on the crews who treated them much as they had their unloaded BAOR counterparts.'

Richard Allen 9/12L

A line of 9th/12th Lancers Centurions tarped up and ready for transport to or from a West German training area in 1968. (*Brian Clarke*)

Moving onto a BAOR tank training area in the late 1960s. The Centurion Mk.6 pictured is still wearing a muzzle cap so this will not be a battle run, but we can see the steep grades and deeply rutted tank route on the training area. (*Brian Clarke*)

Chapter Seven

The Armoured Regiments in the Early Cold War Period

The organisation of the armoured regiments in the 1950s followed the pattern used in 1945. Each regiment in peacetime included a headquarters squadron controlling logistics and administration, a command troop of two or three tanks, a reconnaissance troop of eight Cromwells (and later of sixteen Ferrets) and three sabre squadrons designated A,B and C. Each squadron included a headquarters troop with two or three tanks and the REME's ARV. Twelve more of the squadron's tanks were divided into troops of three or possibly four tanks (if officers were in short supply). The sabre squadrons were commanded by a captain or a major. Each troop was commanded by a lieutenant or a second-lieutenant. A war establishment of fifty-two Centurions in three squadrons was the basis for an armoured regiment in the 1950s.

After the Korean War the reconnaissance troop's Cromwells began to be replaced by Ferret scout cars. In 1955, the Conqueror began to be issued. Much thought went into arming the Conqueror but as the army had never employed such a massive vehicle, its use called for some special considerations. The RAC had no plan how to use heavy tanks and the government did not buy enough Conquerors to keep them in heavy regiments as first intended.[33] The BAOR armoured regiments devised their own methods of employing Conquerors without any standard guideline, and generalised practices developed as a matter of common sense. Most regiments received nine Conquerors, although some only ever received six. At first some regiments split them, with one Conqueror per Centurion troop in each of three squadrons. This was how Sherman Fireflies had been used in the war, but it prevented the Conqueror from being used for heavy fire support. When integrated into Centurion troops, the Conqueror was used the same way as a fourth Centurion, thereby negating all the advantages of having a long range 120mm gun. The best solution was to create heavy troops, keeping three Conquerors together in each Centurion squadron.

Tactics with the Centurion stressed tracking and engaging the enemy on the move using the gun stabilisation system. The Conqueror was over ten tons heavier than the Centurion and could not normally use the standard Centurion Armoured Vehicle Launched Bridge to cross rivers. From a tactical point of view, the Conqueror was supposed to be used as a long range weapon that fired from the halt. It had more than enough firepower to deal with the Stalin

A Conqueror with substantial camouflage. (*B. Griffin*)

Two Conqueror Mk.2s of the 5th Royal Inniskilling Dragoon Guards. B Squadrons' were named *Bewitched*, *Bothered*, and *Bewildered*. The Conqueror had frontal armour as thick as 200mm on the gun mantlet, 130mm on the glacis and turret sides 90mm thick. Its fire control system and gun were designed for destroying enemy tanks at long range. (*Noel McCleery*)

tanks that were so widely feared and the combination was often incompatible – but it did offer the armoured regiment some tactical advantages in a defensive battle.

In the Middle East before the 1960s, the wastes in Cyrenaica were ideal, largely uninhabited manoeuvre areas. In Libya some camps occupied by the army included existing Italian barracks like those at Sabratha and Homs dating back to the 1930s. In North Africa, firing ranges were easily set up and there was plenty of wartime ammunition available to discharge from armoured cars or tanks. In West Germany the training areas of Soltau and Bergen-Hohne were ideally suited to training armoured regiments, but in the early days of BAOR these ranged far and wide – often causing damage to farmland and public roads. After the establishment of the *Bundesrepublic*, German sensibilities became a matter for careful consideration. Finding training areas for squadron or higher level manoeuvres became more difficult outside scheduled training periods in a few areas. From the early 1950s the rapid growth of the RAC presence in Germany required carefully scheduled regimental and brigade level training schemes.

Tactics evolved with weapons, and were practised throughout the year at different levels in both the classroom and the field. Despite actual exercises only occupying a small portion of the year, armoured regiments in BAOR spent much time preparing for unit and formation training periods. It was important to avoid two regiments from the same brigade being away at the same time because that would affect operational readiness. The other considerations in assigning training periods were the means at hand. Transportation had to be arranged with minimal congestion of the West German road and rail system. Tank transporter regiments of the Royal Army Service Corps had to move the tanks with their crews, and even squadron

Track bashing, a hard job for all concerned, was one of the most unpleasant tasks faced by a tank crew. Tank tracks stretched with use, and links were removed to compensate, but eventually a new set of tracks was needed. Here a Centurion Crew from the 16th/5th Lancers is hard at work on the tank park in 1967. (*Geoffrey Wells*)

Infra-red vision capability was an important technological advance for the Centurion, and was retrofitted to the Centurion in the early 1960s. This is a Centurion Mk.11 or Mk.12 of the 16th/5th Lancers on the tank park in 1967; on the right side of the photo we can see a Mk.7 or Mk.8 Centurion. (*Geoffrey Wells*)

On 4 April 1959 there was a parade commemorating the tenth anniversary of NATO's creation, and amongst the British forces representing BAOR were the 1st The Queen's Dragoon Guards. Note how the spearhead emblem of the 1st British Corps is carried on the rear plate of the nearest Saladin. The QDG were corps troops who enjoyed a long career in armoured cars and became Wales' armoured unit – known famously as the Welsh Cavalry. (*Jumbo Harrison*)

1959 also marked the introduction of the Saladin, which replaced the AEC Mk.III. This example was with the QDG. (*Jumbo Harrison*)

level exercises might be coordinated with infantry, or with the Royal Artillery. Each training period was planned to test and perfect aspects of a regiment's ability to go to war at a high state of proficiency. The densely populated 1st British Corps area involved soldiers and civilians living alongside each other and manoeuvres were part of the landscape for over half a century.

Exercises were conducted at corps, division, brigade and regimental levels. The large NATO autumn exercises held each year tested the 1st British Corps' ability to defend its sector, and could involve elements of all the large formations in BAOR. The mission was to counter any offensive by Soviet Ground Forces with counter attacks and staged withdrawals to river lines. Exercises were planned on a two year cycle, so that units could focus on regimental level tactics in one year, and in the next, work with other regiments in brigade-focused tactics. Brigade exercises translated at higher level into divisional or corps exercises. These eventually included more and more units and observers from other NATO armies. Often the officers

A modernized Daimler Dingo photographed during a QDG troop briefing in 1959. The arrival of the 76mm gunned Saladin meant that the armoured car troop could operate without need for a dedicated heavy troop in the squadron, but until sufficient Ferrets were available, the Dingo soldiered on. (Jumbo Harrison)

from RAC units based in the UK were sent to BAOR exercises as observers and as umpires. Exercises became massive affairs involving up to an entire month away from bases. The AFV crews lived in their tanks and armoured cars during these exercises, and, at their conclusion, days could elapse before they returned to their bases.

In the 1960s, many regiments filled winter training periods with adventure and troop level training. The lessons of faraway Malaya were implemented by the addition of an air troop consisting of three helicopters to each headquarters squadron to boost reconnaissance capabilities and soon AFV crewmen were being trained as fully qualified helicopter pilots. The SARO Skeeter and Bell Sioux served in the armoured and armoured car regiments. Despite the vulnerability of these helicopters, the innovation was highly appreciated by regimental commanders.

Armoured car crews from 1st QDG in early 1959. The variety in uniforms and the Sterling 9mm SMG were typical for reconnaissance troops. (*Jumbo Harrison*)

One of the biggest exercises recorded in the 1960s was the corps exercise Spearpoint 1961, which lasted six days and tested the change to the brigade-based tactical organization adopted in BAOR. It was the biggest manoeuvre held since 1954, involving two British divisions in an area of thirty by one hundred and fifty miles. Thirty thousand men took part, including American and *Bundeswehr* troops. The newest technology was used and the local civilians must have stood in awe at the display of military power. The 1st Armoured Division acted as an attacking force, deploying helicopter-borne infantry to take the Weser bridges ahead of an armoured thrust. The 2nd Infantry Division, representing the defenders, mounted a series of counterattacks. Measures were of course taken to keep the amount of damage to the German road system to a minimum, these included leaving all of the participating regiments' Conquerors in their bases (which took away some of the realism), but it was otherwise a grim reminder of what could be expected. By the sixth day of mock combat, both sides were to have resorted to nuclear weapons. For many of the participants this would have been given little consideration amongst the complexities of the exercise.[34]

Based on the experience gained fighting in Malaya, RAC regiments (both armoured and reconnaissance) began to be equipped with air troops in the early 1960s. The air troop consisted of three helicopters under the administration of the regimental HQ Squadron, and the pilots were selected and trained from AFV crewmen serving with the regiment. This SARO Skeeter was on strength of the 9th/12th Lancers in 1967, and carries the regimental badge. (*Brian Clarke*)

A 12th Infantry Brigade Group maintenance crew and pilots of the 9th/12th Lancers checking over a Skeeter in the late 1960s. All carry Sterling SMGs, and, like all webbing in the regiment, the pilot's pistol holster is blancoed brown. (*Richard Allen*)

Westland Wasps of the 12th Infantry Brigade Group in the late 1960s. (*Brian Clarke*)

Annual training within a regiment could be divided into roughly five periods by the late 1960s, demonstrating that the year was one massive series of preparatory stages for relatively brief training periods. Each required a component of training within the regiment, squadron and troop. Each period incorporated the need to teach new personnel many new skills. Tank crews learnt to acquire and accumulate the necessary extras for life on exercise. Experienced troopers taught their younger comrades all the old tricks. A rough idea of training in the 9th/12th Lancers in the late 1960s is shown below.[35]

Jan – Apr	Regimental trade training to basic crewman standard in gunnery, radio operator, driver A (tracked) vehicle or driver B (wheeled) vehicles.
Apr – June	Two weeks of regimental field training on Soltau Training Area.
Jun – July	Two weeks of regimental gunnery practice on Hohne firing ranges.
Aug – Oct	Two weeks of divisional field training exercise over open West German countryside.
Nov – Dec	Preparation for the following year and the start of trade training.

There could be much variation in how a regiment's year might pass depending on how their training periods fitted into the larger training schedule. Some regiments had their different squadrons undertake troop level training earlier in the training year if it suited the availability of training grounds. Training areas were occasionally found in southern France, much to the delight of the regiments concerned! Occasionally, a regiment might exchange a troop with an allied regiment, as the 3rd Carabiniers did with one of the Danish Centurion regiments in

1965. In the 1970s deployments to train in Denmark and Norway became more common.[36]

The British Army's post-war tank designs all used four man crews made up of a commander, a driver, a gunner and a loader/wireless operator. Older designs like the Cromwell and Comet had five man crews, but after the mid-1950s these designs were relegated to units outside of BAOR and they ended as equipment for the Territorial Army. From 1947 until 1962 crewmen included both volunteers and National Service conscripts. Discounting the many other types of reconnaissance AFVs and troop transport vehicles adopted by the RAC in the same period, RAC crewmen in the armoured regiments of BAOR between 1955 and 1965 were either 'Centurion Men' or 'Conqueror Men'. As might be expected, there were many humorous rivalries between them. The men of the armoured cars and of the reconnaissance troops in the armoured regiments had a similar belief in their superiority and that of their equipment, and would have been proving it as regularly as possible in manoeuvres, or on playing fields.

The most visible and dangerous place in the RAC in the Cold War was in an armoured vehicle crew. Men were killed every year during training and soldiering had to be taken very seriously. The Centurion was generally well liked by its crews for its simplicity, reliability and general ease of use. The Conqueror was a far more demanding vehicle to serve on, demanding a specialist approach that it never officially received. Some former crew members have

A hangar scene in an unknown BAOR armoured regiment, and probably one that can be taken as typical for the end of the Conqueror era if this represents a single troop of tanks. Three Centurion Mk.5s are seen with type B 20-pounder barrels (including an early turret vehicle in the foreground) and a lone Conqueror Mk.2 is at the back. Closest to the camera is another Centurion Mk.3 or Mk.5 with the original type of cast turret, a tool box on the roof and a fitter or crewman climbing aboard. (*MP Robinson collection*)

After the 6th RTR and 3rd RTR merged into the 'New 3rd RTR' in 1959 its vehicles included, 02 BB 20, a C Squadron Conqueror Mk.2 named *Chevron*. The Conqueror was never particularly reliable due to its overworked engine, and here a broken down *Chevron* is seen awaiting the ARV in 1962. (*Pete Dobson*)

Chevron's gunner posed in front of his tank in happier circumstances. The Conqueror was a very large and heavy vehicle but might have earned more affection had it ever been used in anger by virtue of its powerful 120mm gun. (*Pete Dobson*)

On exercise it was standard practice to camouflage the tank once its harbour area was selected. It was especially important to prevent identification from the air and much effort went into the ritual of hiding the tank before maintenance and food preparation could begin. The crew would usually fix a tarpaulin to one side of the tank and sleep with some degree of comfort in the makeshift tent this provided. Each man took a guard period while the rest slept. (*Pete Dobson*)

expressed an ironic satisfaction in the Conqueror's poor reliability record because it frequently broke down on exercise (often close to a *Gasthaus*), which could give the crew several days off. The Conquerors spent a great deal of time in their hangars and undergoing maintenance and, by the mid-1960s at the end of their careers, availability was poor.[37]

The Centurion commander was provided with a good view from his cupola and benefitted from a well laid out position with a simple and reliable fire control system. Crew commander training was done within the armoured regiment under the guidance of the troop NCOs and a tank was usually commanded by a lance corporal. That job was a multi-tasking exercise that required full mental attention at all times. With many things going on simultaneously, the crew commander needed a natural sense of responsibility. A tank commander did not fit all personality types: and, with today's simulators unknown, everything had to be learnt on the job. The tank commander had to keep abreast of events within the troop and squadron through the wireless net, remain aware of his location on the map at all times, keep control of his crew and often guide the driver, while keeping his eye out for any potential tactical situations (as well as the provision of fuel, ammunition and rations). Despite the responsibilities, many young tank commanders thrived on the excitement of a tank on manoeuvre and would miss the hustle and bustle of that life in later years.

The crew breakfasted and could be underway after rolling up the camouflage net. (*Pete Dobson*)

The Conqueror's large turret bustle housed the commander's Fire Control Turret. It was specially designed and armed to engage and defeat tanks like the IS-3 and the T-10 that followed, and probably would have dealt with any contemporary battle tank. In British service it was unique in its use of an optical rangefinder. (*Pete Dobson*)

Chieftain commander Rob Jacobs at BATUS during battle group training with 3rd RTR in 1989. The mass of electrical cabling attached to the turret walls is visible. A tank commander was responsible for both the lives of his crew and a complex war machine. (*Rob Jacobs*)

A Centurion Mk.11 being fuelled up with a special funnel that held multiple jerrycans. The Centurion had a petrol engine like many of its contemporaries. Special care was always in order when fuelling because of the risk of fire. (*Brian Clarke*)

A tank turret was a crowded house and teamwork was the key. The Centurion evolved but even three different main armaments in a dozen years did not cause fundamental changes. The gunner's role in both the Centurion and Conqueror was similar although the tanks differed in how the fire control systems functioned and in gunnery drill. Both had controls for power traverse and gun laying, along with hand controls for more precise adjustment. A good gunner was worth his weight in gold, but on the Conqueror the wayward gunner was far enough from the commander's seat to escape the traditional boot in the back that followed a missed shot on the Centurion. Despite the possibility that a gunner might decide the life or death of a tank crew, he was often the youngest man in that crew. In the armoured car regiments gunners were often seventeen or eighteen because no soldier under eighteen was allowed a driver's licence. In other words, they might be too young for anything else!

The loader/wireless operator's role was usually the penultimate step before a crewman was made a vehicle commander. The loader fed the main armament and co-axial machine guns, and maintained them during firing. The Centurion's loader had over fifty rounds of 20-pounder or 105mm ammunition in his care, and if he was good at the job the Centurion could manage two rounds in the air at once. The Conqueror's 120mm gun carried thirty-five two-piece rounds which slowed the rate of fire. The loader kept the radios tuned in and helped the tank commander with messages and decoding. All these tasks were vital to the efficient running of the tank, but there was another duty essential of any loader/operator in the RAC: head cook and bottle washer! The loader usually ended up making hot drinks and cooking in the *boiling*

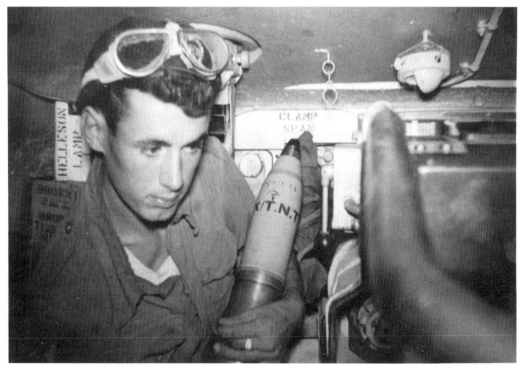

This posed photo was taken inside a Centurion Mk.3's turret in 1956. The loader is Pete Dobson of the 6th RTR who is holding a high explosive 20-pounder round. Some details of the turret interior are visible – then painted silver with stowage locations marked. (*Pete Dobson*)

vessel. This in its simplest form was a saucepan-like container with a heating element that worked like an electric kettle. In armoured cars there were no such luxuries and in the Daimler, AEC and Saladin the crew commander was also the gun loader for the main armament; cooking was done when the crew made camp or by the Army Catering Corps.

The loader had to clear empty casings from the turret, otherwise in action they would have piled up very fast. On the Centurion this was easy because the shell casings fit through the ejection port in the turret side. The Conqueror was a different story: the empty 120mm case was ejected from the breech, but, due to the size of the casing, a mechanical system was devised to remove them from the turret. This shell casing disposal system was known as *the Mollins gear* to the Conqueror's crew, and was designed to ease the loader's burdens. It sadly broke down frequently and many a 120mm casing was thrown through the open loader's hatch on the ranges. Centurion and Conqueror crews, kept busy with constant training, vehicle maintenance and drills, had to function like a well-oiled machine with everyone knowing their duties. Pete Dobson recalls a crew's routine on exercise:

> 'Whenever we stopped for the night my commander, who happened to be the troop officer, went for an orders group, the driver went to see the fitters if he had any mechanical problems, the gunner cammed up the tank, and I prepared the evening meal. These basic tasks varied and sometimes I had to sit in the turret on radio watch, so we all mucked in on whatever there was to do. At night on exercise we all slept in a row in the tank bivouac and took a turn as sentry, so everybody contributed towards the security of the vehicle.'

The tasks the AFV crews shared in any given day could be laborious. Refuelling before the mid-1970s was demanding and involved all four crewmen wherever possible to complete the process quickly. Some forty to sixty jerry cans of petrol would be needed, depending on the tank and mark in question, and each one weighed some forty pounds when full… with a couple of cans of engine oil daily for each tank to boot. These were delivered by the regimental echelon at pre-arranged refuelling points. Until a special funnel designed to hold multiple jerry cans began to be issued in the 1960s, each can was poured in singly, a massive task with a constant risk of fire. Another timeless backbreaker was 'bombing up' the tanks with a full ammunition load. Each task on a tank became a drill practised for the smartest results, sometimes under the watchful eyes of the squadron sergeant-major! Hated chores on a tank involved the tracks which were constantly inspected by the driver; tensioning was always a tough task that involved the whole crew and a giant spanner but this paled compared to the despised 'track bashing' (changing worn tracks) which could take an entire day or more.

A tank driver's visibility was always limited (even in day light with his head out), but at night the risks multiplied tenfold. Many accidents of either spectacular or tragic nature happened in the days of the Centurion and Conqueror in BAOR; driving a tank was then (and remains) a crew task where skill is always prized. Before 1959, when the Phillips infra-red searchlights became available for the Centurion, most manoeuvre activity was confined to daylight. For safety reasons tanks halted in 'harbour areas' on manoeuvres where they would have been guarded by sentries and, theoretically, by infantry. By coincidence many harbour areas were sited close to a *gasthaus.* Sometimes a thorough reconnaissance was performed in advance to assure proximity! After the introduction of infra-red equipment, the whole tempo of manoeuvres changed, and on many occasions tanks equipped with the infra-red sights gave the opposing infantry a thoroughly difficult time in nocturnal exercises! The Conquerors were

Pete Dobson, 6th RTR, trying his hand at driving a Centurion Mk.3. The Centurion had a crash gearbox and changing gears and steering demanded skill and close attention to the engine's RPM. Once the tiring task of operating his tank was over the driver was responsible for checking fluid levels, suspension and tracks, and the engine and gearbox. (*Pete Dobson*)

never fitted with infra-red equipment, nor were the Ferrets of the Reconnaissance Troops, or the Saladins and Ferrets of the Armoured Car Regiments. A squadron's night fighting ability could thus vary in the early 1960s, depending on the equipment in use. It was a sign of things to come, and by the 1970s night vision capability was universal in all RAC regiments. This however never stopped the practice of harbouring near a *gasthaus*.[38]

The arrival of the L7 105mm gun after 1959 increased the Centurion's firepower and some regiments converted all of their Centurions in one year to the new gun. Other regiments converted more slowly. For a short while in the early 1960s the mixture of different guns within a regiment's tank park could be surprising. There were not always enough 105mm guns to replace all the 20-pounder guns in Centurion regiments; conversion could take a long time and the Conquerors were still on strength. This meant that the logistics requirements could include 120mm, 105mm and 20-pounder ammunition to feed three types of tank guns, and possibly also 7.92mm, .30 calibre and .50 calibre ranging munitions for the tanks' machine guns. This logistic nightmare diminished towards the mid-1960s and ended when the Chieftains arrived. The basic crew roles evolved with the Chieftain and Challenger, but only in the details of the functions of the vehicle's armaments. Otherwise little has changed for a tank crew to this day (beyond the technology of the vehicles themselves).

The Royal Armoured Corps was represented in almost every Middle Eastern deployment that the Army undertook in the 1960s. The strong British relationships with Jordan and Iraq

A rare shot of a Centurion Mk.2 being desert tested by the 4th RTR in Libya in 1948. The Centurion was a very rare vehicle outside BAOR at the time and went on to be the iconic British tank of the 1950s and early 1960s. Between 1947 and 1952 the 4th RTR was stationed throughout the Middle East, most often in Palestine and the Suez Canal zone. In 1949, the 4th RTR were the first unit to send a squadron to Aqaba in Jordan. (*Brian Simpson*)

Two Bays troopers in front of an American built halftrack in Libya in 1947. Such halftracks had a long postwar career in the British Army serving as command vehicles and as fitters vehicles in the Royal Armoured Corps; the last of them were replaced in the late 1960s. (*Brian Simpson*)

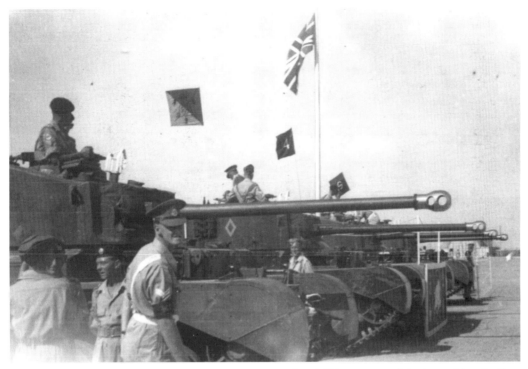

Wearing blancoed webbing and with the muzzle brakes of their 77mm guns polished to a shine, the Bays prepare for the farewell parade when the 1st Armoured Division disbanded at Qassassin, Egypt, in September 1947. The closest tank is a Bays Comet. The 1st Division's white rhino emblem was revived for the 10th Armoured Division, which operated in the area in the following decade. (*Brian Simpson*)

The Hashemite Kingdom of Jordan maintained strong relations with Britain in the early 1950s. British troops still served in Jordan in the mid-1950s to deter conflicts between Israel and Jordan; in 1954 a squadron from the Queen's Bays deployed there. The photo shows an M19 tank transporter with a Bays Centurion aboard. (*Jumbo Harrison*)

The furthest north that the British detachments operated in Jordan was the outpost at Ma'an. Road movements were treacherous at times, and here a tank transporter with a Bays Centurion Mk.3 aboard is negotiating a bend on the rocky path that served as a road. The path led under the bridge in the background which involved passing between the pillars with a loaded M19! (*Jumbo Harrison*)

This photo was probably taken from the bridge after the tank transporters had passed through. The Bays detachment returned to the 10th Armoured Division in Libya in 1956 when the 10th Hussars relieved them in Aqaba. (*Jumbo Harrison*)

The 10th Hussars served as part of Force O (which also included a detached infantry company of the Middlesex Regiment and a battery of artillery) based at Aqaba on the southern tip of Jordanian-Israeli border and later further north at Ma'an. The post at Aqaba had been taken over from The Queen's Bays, who had served in Jordan from November 1954 until the end of 1955. This Centurion Mk.3 is riding on an M19 Diamond T tank transporter. (*Andy Hill*)

A splendid study of an early production Centurion Mk.3 of the 10th Hussars on detachment from the 10th Armoured Division with Force O. The loader's periscope with 2 inch bomb thrower was replaced on the later Mk.3s with a simple periscope located in the sloped turret roof casting. When the 10th Hussars began leaving Jordan in April 1957 they suffered the tragic loss of twenty-three men in an air crash at Quweira. (*Andy Hill*)

A Centurion Mk.3 of the 10th Hussars photographed in the Jordanian desert in 1956. The 10th Hussars were sent back to Britain in April 1957 – a change from the original plan to send the regiment to Barce with other elements of the 10th Armoured Division. Suez was a catalyst for a large scale reduction of the army in the late 1950s including the disbandment of the 10th Armoured Division. (*Andy Hill*)

in the first half of the 1950s were considered vital pillars of foreign policy, but, by the early 1960s the British presence in the Middle East had diminished. The nationalist character of the new Iraq government was decidedly anti-British and eventually forced Britain to protect Kuwait from the menace of Iraqi invasion in 1961 with a force that included Centurions from the 3rd Carabiniers. Libya was long a postwar base for the RAC and keeping bases in the area, once the army left Egypt in 1955, was considered vital. This was confirmed in the aftermath of the Suez Canal crisis and Libya remained an important training base until 1969. In southern Arabia there was also a long series of squadron sized deployments for different regiments; these usually lasted a year and were often followed by a year in Tidworth on training duties.[39]

Aden, between 1960 and 1967, was regularly home to detached armoured car squadrons from several regiments and to detached squadrons of Centurions. When the 16th/5th Lancers deployed B Squadron to Aden in 1963, they came with new Centurion Mk.10s while the rest of the regiment took up stations in Hong Kong and Singapore (C Squadron joined them later in the year). The detached Persian Gulf Squadron operated continuously from landing craft and was liable for service throughout the whole southern Arabian peninsular. Troops of armoured

A reconnaissance or liaison Ferret Mk.1 in Libya in 1956 with the 6th Royal Tank Regiment. (*Pete Dobson*)

A squadron laager in the Libyan Desert in 1956. 6th RTR was involved in the area and participated in Operation Musketeer in Egypt in the same period. (*Pete Dobson*)

The desert has always encouraged individualism and here is a very rare FV420 trials vehicle with its driver in a rather unusual take on the official uniform! (*Pete Dobson*)

The despised monotrailer with its 200 gallon fuel capacity was perhaps less of a disaster in the desert on good ground. It could be ejected from the interior of the vehicle. The 6th RTR was based at the time in Homs, Libya. (*Pete Dobson*)

The emergency in Cyprus in June 1957 brought a squadron of 6th RTR Centurions to the island. This 1958 photo shows part of a Centurion crew. (*Peter Dobson*)

Men of 42 Royal Marine Commandos loaded aboard 6th RTR Centurions in Cyprus, 1958. (*Pete Dobson*)

The armoured monowheel fuel trailer was a nuisance to use and was reviled amongst Centurion crewmen as the Mollins Gear would be hated by Conqueror crewmen. This photo taken in Cyprus in 1958 shows a 6th RTR Centurion that reversed over its monowheel trailer. The trailer dropped into a deep hole unseen by the crew and became trapped under the Centurion. (*Pete Dobson*)

The 3rd Carabiniers, then stationed at Tidworth deployed the entire regiment (less B Squadron at Warminster) to Kuwait to deter an Iraqi invasion from July until October 1961. This photo, taken on the last day of the Kuwait deployment, shows a Centurion Mk.8 and two sun tanned Carabiniers. (*Gary Rathke*)

RAC South Arabia 1956–70

Regiment	Station	arrival	departure	role
Life Guards (A Sqn)	Aden	Jul-55	Apr-56	armoured car
15th/19th King's Royal Hussars	Aden	Apr-56	Jun-57	armoured car
13th/18th Royal Hussars (Queen Mary's Own) (B Sqn)	Aden	Oct-57	Sep-58	armoured car
Life Guards	Aden and Oman	Sep-58	Nov-59	armoured car
1st The Royal Dragoons	Aden/Sharjah	Nov-59	Dec-60	armoured car
3rd Carabiniers (Prince of Wales's Dragoon Guards) (C Sqn)	Bir Fuqum Camp, Little Aden	Nov-60	Nov-61	Centurion
Queen's Own Hussars (C Sqn)	Persian Gulf LST	Feb-60	Dec-60	amphibious trials
11th Hussars (Prince Albert's Own)	Little Aden/Sharjah	Nov-60	Jun-61	armoured car
Queen's Royal Irish Hussars	Sharjah	Sep-61	Sep-62	armoured car
17th/21st Lancers (HQ,A, B Sqns)	Aden Falaise Lines/Gulf LST	Oct-61	Oct-62	Centurion
9th/12th Royal Lancers (Prince of Wales's)	Little Aden/Sharjah	Sep-62	Jul-63	armoured car
Royal Scots Greys (A+B Sqns)	Aden Falaise Lines/Gulf LST	Oct-62	Nov-63	Centurion
4th Royal Tank Regiment	Little Aden, Sharjah, Radfan	Aug-63	Aug-64	armoured car
16th/5th The Queen's Royal Lancers (HQ, B, C Sqns)	Aden Falaise Lines/Gulf LST	Nov-63	Dec-64	Centurion
10th Royal Hussars (Prince of Wales's Own)	Little Aden/Sharjah	Aug-64	Aug-65	armoured car
9th/12th Royal Lancers (Prince of Wales's)	Aden	Aug-64	Aug-65	Centurion
5th Royal Inniskilling Dragoon Guards	Aden Falaise Lines/Gulf LST	Dec-64	Dec-65	Centurion
4th/7th Royal Dragoon Guards	Little Aden/Sharjah	Aug-65	Aug-66	armoured car
1st Royal Tank Regiment (HQ,A, C Sqns)	Aden Falaise Lines/Gulf LST	Dec-65	Jan-67	Centurion*
1st Queen's Dragoon Guards	Aden: Mareth Lines, Falaise Lines, Little Aden, Sharjah	Sep-66	Jul-67	armoured car
5th Royal Tank Regiment (B Sqn)	Aden	Apr-67	Jul-67	armoured car
3rd Royal Tank Regiment (B Sqn)	Sharjah	Jan-68	Dec-68	armoured car
Life Guards (A Sqn)	Sharjah	Oct-69	Jun-70	armoured car

* included two Chieftain Mk.2 on trials

cars or Centurions could be detached to Bahrain, Muskat, or into the Radfan area as required. In Aden the local population was extremely restive, the risk of terrorist attack was high and the RAC sustained frequent casualties. Facilities were primitive and remote.

> 'Little Aden Cantonment, or Falaise Camp as it is called, is difficult to describe. Situated some twenty-five miles from Aden and connected to Aden by what can truthfully be called the most dangerous road in the Middle East...'[40]

For armoured cars the greatest risk came from mines or ambush on convoy escort. The 10th Hussars, for example, had three Saladins, twelve Ferrets and a Scammell recovery tractor mined in Aden between August 1964 and September 1965. The main purpose for the Centurions deployed in southern Arabia and Aden, was to serve as infantry support or long range artillery. Amphibious landings were regularly practised on the coastal areas until the British presence in Aden ended in 1967. With that passed an era of strategic focus on the Middle East that had lasted since the Suez Canal was built.[41]

A Saladin of N.7 Troop, A Squadron 4th RTR at Wadi Manawa. This troop, commanded by Lieutenant Mike Rose, saw frequent action. Mines were a big problem; this vehicle is receiving a substitute Saracen wheel assembly after a Teller mine blew off the front left wheel. Major George Forty commanded A Squadron in the Radfan during the last months of 1963 until February 1964, when the decision was taken to pull back units stationed in the eastern Radfan. (*4th RTR Association with thanks to Major-General Sir Lawrence New*)

The 16th/5th Lancers served in Aden in 1963, with A Squadron detached to Hong Kong and B and C Squadrons rotating between garrison duties and manning the Persian Gulf LST Squadron. The 16th/5th Lancers were the first to fire the new L7 105mm gun in action and their Centurions wore some of the most striking camouflage schemes. This is a Mk.10 but photos show that the regiment also had Mk.9s and Mk.6s at the time. (*Copyright Dusty Terry/The Lancers' Dropbox Media Group*)

A line of Centurion Mk.6s of B Squadron, 5th Royal Inniskilling Dragoon Guards in the tank park at Little Aden in early 1965. Unlike many of the Aden-based Centurions, these vehicles lack the commonly seen black or dark green disruptors. The white recognition stripes on the rear hull were standard on Aden-based Centurions and none have the long range tank fitted. (*Noel McLeery*)

A lineup of Centurion Mk.6s of the 5th Inniskilling Dragoon Guards in Aden in 1965. (*Noel McLeery*)

A and B Squadrons of the 5th Inniskilling Dragoon Guards rotated between Falaise Lines, Aden, and the Persian Gulf squadron permanently stationed on LSTs in the Persian Gulf. During that period the LST Squadron tended to carry late model Centurions while those stationed at little Aden included some rebuilt older model vehicles – but all were by then armed with the deadly 105mm gun. (*Noel McLeery*)

Landing operations were normally supported by a Centurion BARV, seen here on standby while Centurions manned by the 5th Inniskilling Dragoon Guards come ashore. There was some variation in the camouflage carried by these tanks, but all carry the white recognition stripe markings. (*Noel McCleery*)

Thumier, Radfan, April 1965. A Saladin of the 10th Hussars with its ammunition load. The Saladin was well armed with a 76mm gun and, firing HESH rounds, could theoretically have knocked out any light tank in Warsaw Pact service. (*Peter Hill*)

The 1966 White Paper, prepared under the direction of secretary of state for defence Denis Healey set the blueprint for Britain's final withdrawal from nearly all its remaining colonial military commitments. It also set NATO as Britain's defence priority. BAOR headquarters moved to Rheindalen, the headquarters of 1st British Corps to Bielefeld, and the three nominal divisions all established headquarters that could be activated in the event of war. Between 1968 and 1971 the army again decreased in size and more armoured regiments had to amalgamate or disappear. The entire corps was affected. In 1969, the 5th RTR was disbanded and six cavalry regiments were amalgamated to form three. The 10th Hussars and 11th Hussars (who had only received the first Chieftains a few years earlier) were amalgamated into The Royal Hussars (the Prince of Wales's Own). In the same year the Royal Horse Guards and 1st The Royal Dragoons amalgamated into The Blues and Royals. 1971 saw the final amalgamations for the Royal Armoured Corps during the Cold War as the 3rd Carabiniers amalgamated with the Royal Scots Greys to form the Royal Scots Dragoon Guards (or SCOTS DG).[42]

A Centurion Mk.11 of the 2nd RTR bogged on a snowy German training area in the winter of 1966–67. (*Dorian Llewellyn*)

Chapter Eight

Armoured Reconnaissance

When the RAC was formed in 1939 from the cavalry regiments and the battalions of the Royal Tank Regiment, the cavalry were replacing horses with armoured cars. Wheeled armour already had a long and successful history in the British Army predating the tank. During the Second World War the armoured car regiment was the corps unit considered to be the eyes of the army. The role was refined after the war by the Royal Armoured Corps and, by 1954, in BAOR a corps armoured car regiment was bolstered by a divisional reconnaissance regiment in each armoured divisions. The armoured reconnaissance role only gained in importance in the next decade, and, between 1957 and 1970, two (and at times three) armoured reconnaissance regiments served under the 1st British Corps.

Work was dangerous in the armoured reconnaissance regiments, mainly because armoured car regiments were amongst the first sent to areas of unrest outside BAOR. They kept the peace in a low key manner impossible for tanks, showed the flag and maintained order, while supporting infantry and protecting supply lines. In the late 1940s all wartime vehicles, including American designs, were retained as standard equipment. Britain had produced a range of fine armoured cars during the war of which the best were standardized and retained into the 1950s. These vehicles included the Daimler Armoured Car, Daimler Dingo Scout Car and the AEC Armoured Car Mk. III.

From the late 1950s the Daimler Ferret Scout Car, Alvis Saracen Armoured Personnel Carrier and the Alvis Saladin Armoured Car replaced the old wartime vehicles. The Malayan Emergency was heavily supported by RAC units in the armoured car role and accelerated development of these new vehicles. Eventually, five RAC regiments equipped with Daimler armoured cars, Ferrets and Saracens served in Malaya. The 12th Lancers joined the 13th/18th Hussars from 1951 until 1954. In 1953 the 13th/18th Hussars were relieved from their first tour by the 11th Hussars who stayed until 1956. From 1954 to 1957, the 15/19th Hussars operated in Malaya in turn. By 1956, with the situation in Malaya coming under control, the armoured cars were operating throughout the colony escorting convoys and keeping order (including operations in Singapore). From 1956 the 15th/19th Hussars were joined by the King's Dragoon Guards, and the Malayan commitment slowly shrank. The KDG stayed until relieved in 1958 by the 13/18th Hussars. The Lilywhites' second tour lasted until 1961 when most of the British troops departed. In Malaya the British Army developed much of its guerrilla warfare doctrine and, for the armoured cars, it was a war of ambushes. The greatest lesson

Vehicles of the 13th/18th Hussars parked at the barracks at Wolfenbuttel in 1946 show some of the key elements of an armoured car squadron from the Second World War. *Ballasalla* and *Betty* were Daimler Armoured Car Mk.Is used in the armoured car troops alongside Dingo scout cars The CT15s were Canadian built armoured lorries used to carry the Assault Troop or as armoured ambulances; the M3 Scout Car was used as a command vehicle or in the Assault Troop. *(John Jolivet)*

from the campaign was the value of the spotter plane and subsequently that of the helicopter, which was integrated into the armoured and armoured reconnaissance regiments for the rest of the 1960s.[43]

The cavalry was assigned the armoured car role exclusively until 1956, when the Royal Tank Regiment also took on the light armoured role for the first time since 1939. In the 1960s wheeled AFVs continued to be employed in peace keeping and in the maintenance of order in trouble spots. They were far better suited than tanks to the problems of urban guerrilla tactics and convoy escort. Wherever a low profile army presence was required, either for peacekeeping or against guerrillas, armoured cars provided the infantry with secure

After the 13th/18th Hussars returned from Malaya in July 1953 they trained as a reconnaissance regiment and, in November, joined the 11th Armoured Division at Wolfenbuttel in West Germany. In 1956 they became a 1st British Corps armoured car regiment based at Neumunster. This Dingo named *Cold Mist* was a C Squadron vehicle during their tour with the 11th Armoured Division and carries the standard smoke dischargers retrofitted also to Daimler Armoured Cars and to the AEC Mk.III. (*Ivor Pollington*)

This Daimler Armoured Car Mk.II *Chelsea* of C Squadron, the 13th/18th Hussars was photographed in its hangar in Wolfenbuttel. (*Ivor Pollington*)

The AEC Armoured Car Mk.III had been one of the most powerfully armoured cars of the Second World War and remained amongst the best armed vehicles of its type into the late 1950s. Known as Matadors by the 1950s, these cars served in the heavy troop of each armoured car squadron. In the 13th/18th Hussars the heavy troops consisted of two Matadors and one American halftrack along with an Austin Champ or Willis Jeep. (*Ivor Pollington*)

The AEC Armoured Car Mk.III was somewhat underpowered and suffered more frequent breakdowns than the smaller Daimler vehicles. This vehicle belonging to the C Squadron Heavy Troop was named *Catterick*, and presumably had developed a fault of some kind when photographed. Two White Scout Cars used by the assault troop are in the background. (*Ivor Pollington*)

When the 13th/18th Hussars took on the corps armoured car role in April 1956 they received a number of Little John squeeze bore devices for the 2-pounder guns of their Daimler Armoured Cars. The role of corps armoured car regiment included border patrols. (*Ivor Pollington*)

A camouflaged AEC Armoured Car Mk.III (bearing the spear badge of the 1st British Corps on its mudguard) of the 13th/18th Hussars C Squadron heavy troop in 1956 or 1957. (*Ivor Pollington*)

This Dingo was named *St Cyprian* – in keeping with the tradition of C Squadron vehicles carrying names starting with the letter C. (*Ivor Pollington*)

Stopped in front of a *gasthaus* on the border between West and East Germany in 1957, these two 13th/18th Hussars Daimler Armoured Cars carry the Little John device that improved the muzzle velocity and antitank performance of the 2-pounder gun. (*Ivor Pollington*)

Armoured car crewmen taking a rest on the hull and turret of a little Daimler Armoured Car in 1957. The 2-pounder gun barrel is fitted with the Little John device. (*Ivor Pollington*)

A Ferret Scout Car Mk2 of the 9th/12th Lancers reconnaissance troop on exercise in Germany in 1967. (*Richard Allen*)

A Saladin of No.3 Troop, A Squadron 1st The Queen's Dragoon Guards at checkpoint Bravo, Sheikh Othman in April 1967. The QDG deployed in support of the Royal Anglian Regiment in Aden in 1967 and were among the last RAC units to serve in the area. April 4th 1967 saw engagements involving the QDG's armoured cars and the 3rd Anglians around Sheik Othman police station. In June 1967 the QDG were involved in intensive fighting, in Crater and elsewhere in Aden, against both terrorists and the Aden Armed Police. (*Brian Harrington Spier*)

When this photo was taken in April 1967 the troopers of No.3 Troop, A Squadron QDG and the men of the 3rd Royal Anglian Regiment had spent a sleepless night on the lookout for unrest. Note the Saracen in the foreground carries a roll of barbed wire on the front engine louvres. The QDG were a largely Welsh regiment by the late 1960s and remain so today. (*Brian Harrington Spier*)

A Ferret of A Squadron QDG in Aden in April 1967 – note how the mudguards and stowage bins have been removed. A few months later on 20 June 1967 the regiment was involved in heavy fighting to rescue the pilot of a downed Sioux Air Troop Helicopter. By June 21st the serious situation required Crater to be evacuated temporarily and only night patrols could be undertaken. Crater was retaken on 3 July by the Argylls and QDG after several days of rioting; the QDG left Aden in late July. (*Brian Harrington Spier*)

The infantry in Aden used 'pigs', extemporized armoured lorries, because they minimized sniper casualties although their vulnerability to mines could still not be ignored. These belonged to the 3rd Anglians and were photographed as part of a mobile group made up of D Company, 3rd Royal Anglian Regiment and A Squadron QDG. The soldiers are exhausted from sixteen hours on high alert. (*Brian Harrington Spier*)

communications and the ability for a quick response to trouble. Armoured car regiments served in Aden and in the smaller Persian Gulf states until the final British withdrawal in 1968.[44] When the situation in Ulster in 1969 spun out of control, the Royal Armoured Corps deployments took to the armoured car as the best means of patrolling the countryside. This new role in Ulster came as plans were laid to replace wheeled reconnaissance vehicles with the Combat Vehicle Reconnaissance (Tracked) family from Alvis.

A lesser known role for the armoured car regiments was as an escort for nuclear artillery; this was an RAC responsibility in the 1960s. After Britain adopted the Corporal and Honest John missiles in the late 1950s and deployed these road-bound tactical nuclear systems, armoured car escorts were a necessity. The vulnerability of the Honest John to wartime ambush by special forces was a serious risk. The armoured car regiment became a rotating assignment in the second half of the 1950s (much like the Training Regiment RAC). All the armoured regiments that took on the role needed to adjust to a mentality where stealth and speed took precedence over all other factors.

The wartime armoured car squadron consisted of four sabre troops of two scout cars and two armoured cars, a heavy troop of 75mm armed halftracks or heavy armoured cars, and an assault troop of four armoured personnel carriers (usually White Scout Cars, Half Tracks or armoured lorries). These were commanded from a squadron headquarters troop with a command vehicle, a couple of scout cars, an armoured ambulance and a light aid detachment. It was with this organization that most of the early postwar police actions and interventions in former colonies were conducted. In the mid-1950s a new generation of vehicles began to appear, so that by the early 1960s the armoured car squadron comprised four sabre troops (each of two Ferrets and two Saladins), an assault troop of four Saracens, a headquarters

A CVR(T) Scorpion of the 9/12L uses a German farmer's outbuildings during a Divisional exercise. (*Richard Allen*)

A CVR(T) Scorpion of the 9/12L hiding on a German farm. The Medium Recce Squadron was tasked with reconnaissance by stealth rather than fighting. (*Richard Allen*)

The result of a Coloured Smoke Grenade attack on a CVR(T) Scorpion of the 9th/12th Lancers. (*Richard Allen*)

The Striker Swingfire launcher added punch to Medium Recce squadrons in the 1980s. (*R. Griffin*)

CVR(T)s of the 3rd RTR's Reconnaissance Troop in the early 1980s under camouflage nets. (*Dick Taylor*)

troop with two Ferrets and a Saracen command vehicle, and an armoured ambulance and light aid detachment. Firepower was bolstered by guided missile equipped armoured cars as required, and helicopters could be attached as an integral regimental air troop to increase reconnaissance capabilities. Depending on how an armoured car regiment was employed, the squadron could serve a larger formation in the reconnaissance role or could be assigned missions as a complete regiment.

The introduction of the Combat Vehicle Reconnaissance (Tracked), (or CVR(T) family) in the mid-1970s transformed the armoured car regiments into medium reconnaissance regiments. The Saladin and Saracen disappeared and were replaced with the new aluminium armoured Scorpion and Scimitar tracked reconnaissance vehicles. These speedy and nimble six tonners brought new capabilities and simplified maintenance. The CVR(T) family included the Spartan APC, the Samson ARV, the Sultan command vehicle and the Striker antitank vehicle armed with five Swingfire antitank missiles. Armoured reconnaissance regiments became more flexible, less road-bound and much more heavily armed. Equipped with the whole family of CVR(T)s, several different orders of battle for this type of unit existed as equipment and roles evolved in the last ten years of the Cold War.

The basic sabre troop in a medium reconnaissance squadron consisted of two Scimitars (the troop leader and troop sergeant) and two Scorpions (commanded by two troop corporals). Early in 1984 the squadron structure changed when twelve Striker Swingfire launcher vehicles were issued to each BAOR medium reconnaissance regiment. A guided weapons troop was added to each squadron at the expense of a sabre troop. The redundant

127

Stealth and observation were critical – a Chieftain cupola crewman on watch in the 1980s. (*Dick Taylor*)

A Striker under test at Chertsey in the early 1980s. The Striker offered the Medium Reconnaissance Squadron a powerful antitank capability in the Armoured Reconnaissance Regiments after 1984. (*Brian Clarke*)

The Striker, like the Scorpion and Scimitar, exerted minimal ground pressure and could cross boggy terrain very well. The tradeoff for the CVR(T)'s weight was thin aluminum armour, which only afforded protection from rifle calibre bullets. Their Jaguar petrol engine enabled them to reach seventy miles per hour on a metalled road – thus stealth and speed provided their best chances of survival. (*Brian Clarke*)

An FV101 CVR(T) Scorpion on the Soltau ranges in 1985. (*Bob Girling*)

The Spartan was the APC variant of the CVR(T) family seen here in company of an FV434 of the squadron LAD in 1985. (*Bob Girling*)

Belize was one of the CVR(T)'s more exotic haunts. Here a crew of the 16th/5th Lancers prepare for a hot, sweaty and difficult track bash – even the CVR(T) could shed a track. (*The Lancers' Dropbox Media Group*)

The Fox also served in the Territorial Army – this example from the late 1970s or early eighties shows it with members of the Kent and Sharpshooters Yeomanry. (*Kent and Sharpshooters Yeomanry Museum*)

The Fox served for two decades from 1974 until 1993. It replaced the Ferret and Saladin and mounted the powerful 30mm RARDEN cannon but its one drawback was that it was top heavy and could flip if manoeuvring violently at speed or rounding sharp corners. This example was photographed serving with the Kent and Sharpshooters Yeomanry. (*Kent and Sharpshooters Yeomanry Museum*)

sabre troops were used to create a third medium reconnaissance squadron in each regiment. Consequently a Type A Medium Reconnaissance Regiment deployed two or three medium reconnaissance squadrons of twenty CVR(T) vehicles each, and forty Daimler Foxes in the Close Reconnaissance Squadron.

The major exception to the preference for tracked reconnaissance vehicles was the Fox Combat Vehicle Reconnaissance (Wheeled), or CVR(W), a four wheeled armoured car. The Fox equipped infantry reconnaissance platoons and the RAC's close reconnaissance squadrons (as well as the TA Yeomanry armoured squadrons); it was a descendant of the Ferret Mk.4 and mounted a 30mm RARDEN cannon in a two man turret like the Scimitar. Each close reconnaissance squadron had forty Foxes in five troops of eight vehicles, which were ideal vehicles for securing road networks. The armoured reconnaissance regiments of the late Cold War period were large in terms of vehicles, each with some eighty to a hundred AFVs. They were designed to fight as detached units assigned to battle groups to create maximum flexibility. The real weaknesses were that these regiments were too lightly armed

This photo was probably posed but shows the never ending battle with tracks fought by every tank crew. This is P2, a very early automotive test bed for the Chieftain project at MVEE Chertsey. It retains the Centurion idler wheel and Centurion top roller layout and the lowered suspension. These would change dramatically as the project evolved into the production Chieftain. (*Brian Clarke*)

This is a Chieftain prototype in its second life at MVEE Chertsey after the original trials. The Chieftain had a long development process but was not equipped with a reliable engine until it had been in service for nearly fifteen years. (*Brian Clarke*)

A view from the rear of the same vehicle being tested. The staff at MVEE formed a crucial part of the Royal Armoured Corps history. They were constantly trying and testing technology to provide British tank crews with cutting edge weapons. (*Brian Clarke*)

(and too lightly armoured) to fight for information – a problem that was never resolved during the Cold War.

The British Army endeavoured to keep ahead of tank development in other countries throughout the 1950s and early 1960s. In 1951 a programme called Medium Gun Tank No.2 was instituted. The year may seem premature in hindsight but no one in 1951 could have foreseen the development of the Centurion into a 105mm armed vehicle within the decade. The need for a future tank was dictated by technological arms race between NATO and the USSR – one premised on smaller NATO forces ranged against larger numbers. For this reason the cornerstone of 1950s NATO battle doctrine was the use of battlefield nuclear weapons, and the Centurion and Conqueror predated concepts like crew Nuclear, Biological and Chemical (NBC) protection. The Centurion had been accepted with reservations at higher levels because Soviet heavy tanks always seemed a formidable enemy. The introduction of anti-tank guided missiles into the Soviet arsenal in the 1960s coincided with technological advances that finally allowed the Main Battle Tank to replace Medium Gun Tanks and Heavy Gun Tanks. When the big Conquerors were withdrawn in 1966 one era ended and another began.

The 11th Hussars were the first Chieftain regiment – one of their Mk.2s is seen here in 1967. (*Brian Clarke*)

An early Chieftain Mk.2 without the thermal sleeve on the gun. (*Brian Clarke*)

The rear view of the same vehicle. Note that a civilian seems to be standing in the loaders hatch. Some of the early Chieftains had colourful markings reminiscent of the 1950s. By the early 1970s this smart appearance had disappeared in favour of the black and NATO green camouflage that became a familiar trait on most British AFVs until recent times. (*Brian Clarke*)

Chapter Nine

Chieftain

The Chieftain prototypes began to appear in 1959, equipped with a multifuel engine built by Leyland, and the Chieftain entered production in 1965 before the engine was completely proven. The 11th Hussars started to receive the new tank from November 1966, and the process of converting the armoured regiments to the new tank continued over the next eight years. The Chieftain was designed to be an all-rounder: it had excellent armour, its L11 120mm gun was the most powerful in service anywhere. The driver sat in a supine position in the middle of the sloped glacis and the turret featured a pointed front casting that did away with a traditional mantlet. It had NBC protection and infra-red sights as standard – and with a diesel engine, longer range and lower risk of fire than older designs. Its two piece ammunition used bagged propellant charges that were stowed in water jacketed ammunition bins for survivability.[45]

The Chieftain replaced the Centurion completely during the early 1970s but the process was difficult and the new tank's relative complexity required more crew training. The technology was a mixture of proven and unproven features, and cost controls imposed on the army in the 1970s prevented a quick resolution of its teething troubles. Despite being faster than the Centurion or the Conqueror, the 56-ton vehicle was underpowered and earned a bad reputation for breakdowns through to the 1980s. Technologically the Chieftain ushered in a whole new era and in many ways the character of the RAC's armoured regiments in BAOR changed with it. The jump from the simple and reliable Centurion to the Chieftain was a large one:

'They were like chalk and cheese – the difference was immense! On Centurions, I spent time (as a gunner) polishing the main armament, even brassoing the breech block! On the Chieftain there was no time for such frivolity. All crew members were involved with keeping it on the road – and it was permanent maintenance, hard graft and continual service and repair. Obviously this was the result of it being new, and more sophisticated, for although the .50 Ranging Gun had appeared on later Centurions, we still needed much training on the new sights (and of course) the 120mm gun. The big difference was that there were no more hot brass shell cases to expel from the turret, just a small vent tube remaining after each round of split ammo was fired. Loaders became very proficient at loading projectile and bag charge at speed, whilst making a "brew" of tea and using any

A Chieftain Mk.2 of the 4th/7th RDG used in a training film in 1971. The vehicle commander talking to his driver is Major David Chappell OC of A Squadron 4/7DG. He is wearing high leather boots known as tank park boots. These were only (legally) allowed to be worn by officers. (*R. Griffin*)

A troop of Deep Bronze Green Chieftain Mk.2s in the first days of the Chieftain's career in the 4th/7th RDG – most likely at Hohne. (*R. Griffin*)

Cambrai, a uniquely camouflaged Chieftain of Headquarters Squadron (in fact the commanding officer's tank) of 3rd RTR in 1979. The crew is with *Bundeswehr* observers – typical for manoeuvres of the later Cold War period. (*Rob Jacobs*)

Unofficial artwork on *Cambrai*, HQ Squadron Command Troop, 3rd RTR, 1979. '*Chipmunks are Go*' was a song by Madness at the time, and crewman Rob Jacobs took a tin of coloured chalks on exercise and added this temporary marking to what was already a uniquely camouflaged Chieftain! Given that *Cambrai* was the regimental commanding officer's tank some officers were clearly more tolerant than others! (*Rob Jacobs*)

Cambrai bogged down on the Hohne Impact range prior to Soltau training in 1979. One feature that identified this as a command tank was the twin V antennae for the VRC 321 HF wireless set on which the crew listened to the late great John Peel's show on the BBC World Service (whilst sometime sipping Jagermeister)! (*Rob Jacobs*)

A crew packed their equipment on exercise according to personal taste; here camouflage nets rolled in hessian sheet have been stowed on the NBC pack, but squashed down to permit use of the cupola's rearmost episcopes. Brackets to hold supplementary jerry cans of oil were also added on the rear hull. Anyone protesting such individualism was in contravention to the service manual stowage diagram might have been reminded that this was the 3rd RTR'S commanding officer's tank! The crewman is wearing a British Warm. (*Rob Jacobs*)

In 1968, the *Scarlet and Green Journal* reported favourably of the Chieftain's reliability and mourned its lack of a heater. The lack of a heater was a long standing complaint, whereas talk of the Chieftain's reliability proved very brief! This is a brand new Chieftain Mk.2 photographed in 1968–1969 once the 16th/5th Lancers returned to BAOR. (*Geoffrey Wells*)

The complex Chieftain was at first a disappointment to some crewmen used to the simple and effective Centurion, but it introduced features that perpetuated the Centurion's balance of firepower and protection for another three decades. Mechanical reliability took nearly a decade and a half to achieve. (*Geoffrey Wells*)

empty bag charge bins to keep the cans of beer cool (especially in the heat of summer at Hohne)! With the introduction of Tank Laser Sight came more training, and .50 calibre ranging gun techniques were thereafter referred to as 'steam gunnery'. It still came in very handy if and when a laser fault developed. Overall, the Chieftain was a huge improvement, its major fault being (in the early years) having a grossly underpowered and unreliable power pack.'

John Webster, SCOTS DG

Of its reliability, the following account should be held as very typical (at least until the early 1980s):

'My first large scale exercise in BAOR was in late 1979, after we had been posted from being the demonstration squadron at Warminster back to Paderborn. I'm pretty sure it was a 3rd Armoured Division exercise called Eternal Triangle. I was in the Command Troop, on the commanding officer's tank call sign 0D. That is how the training build up progressed with troop level training at the start of the year (including annual firing at the Hohne Ranges), followed by battle group training... then on to BATUS which I know we did in 1979. In the autumn the training year came to an end with a divisional Field Training Exercise (FTX). We deployed late at night travelling to the exercise area by road, and I can remember on the move out we were passing Chieftain after Chieftain that had broken down on the way. I seem to recall that most of the ones we passed were from the SCOTS DG, which is not to say those in our regiment were any more reliable. Our tank succumbed sometime during the road march, and I woke up in the daylight in what was known as 'the graveyard'. This was basically a REME collection point for broken down tanks, where they were either patched up or had major assemblies changed. It really did look like a graveyard and it was rather sad actually. I don't think we had much more in the way of problems through the rest of that FTX, but it always seemed to me that once you ran the Chieftain for some distance and accepted the inevitable breakdown it would somehow settle down and perform much better thereafter.'

Rob Jacobs, 3rd RTR

Like the Centurion, the Chieftain developed through a whole range of improved versions, and by the mid-1980s it had progressed through eleven different marks. Improvements were made to its fire controls, gun and ammunition, and the whole Chieftain fleet went through many rebuilds to improve engine reliability. The last of these changes were embodied in the Chieftain Mk.10 and Mk.11, which both featured Stillbrew appliqué armour. The Mk.11 also was fitted with TOGS thermal gunnery equipment which gave it true night fighting capability similar to that of the Challenger 1. One of the Chieftain's finer hours came when the 16th/5th Lancers won the Canadian Army Trophy in 1975. At the time of its introduction and even over a decade later, the Chieftain was the most powerful MBT in the world. Nearly every RAC regiment served at some point on the Chieftain by the end of the Cold War.[46]

A Chieftain Mk.2 with unit modified front splashboard and a new Chieftain Mk.5 of the 5th Inniskilling Dragoon Guards awaiting replenishment in West Germany in 1972. As delivered, the Chieftain Mk.2 lacked a front splash board to keep ice and other debris from riding up the glacis plate and the example seen has one of the most common modifications locally added in the late 1960s by regimental workshops. Another such modification of Chieftain Mk.2s was to add the turret bustle bin from derelict M47s or the stowage baskets from Centurions by then being used as range targets. (*Noel McLeery*)

The Chieftain changed considerably between the original Mk.2 issued at the end of 1966, the Mk.3 of 1970 and the Mk.5 of 1972–1973. One of the more visible features was the late style NBC system on the turret rear, as well as the adoption of larger turret baskets, the commander's stowage bin introduced with the Mk.3, and the Infra-Red headlamps and factory splashboard. (*Noel McCleery*)

Chapter Ten

The 1970s

The 1970s began for the RAC with the unfolding tragedy of the Troubles and the national economy in decline. The middle of the decade saw a severe energy crisis limiting the Army's fuel consumption. Amalgamations in the RAC gave the decade a bitter start, with the continuation of the military reduction from the 1960s. The dream of a powerful corps with four armoured divisions in West Germany had not died in the 1970s – but security at home prevented the rationalisation of the Royal Armoured Corps into a wholly NATO-focused role. For the RAC regiments in West Germany there was little variety other than the changing training periods. A range of inspections and other activities designed to keep the men busy were devised, and some of these were viewed with a degree of cynicism by the average soldier. One was the ever present threat of Exercise Quick Train (later renamed Active Edge) being called.

Quick Train was designed to test operational readiness of units and was conducted for years. It was always described in glowing terms in regimental journals but, to the trooper and the NCO, it was seen as a fraud on a grand scale. Armoured regiments would be warned when they were entering a period of being liable for call out under *Quick Train;* and regimental vehicles were fully kitted out and all troops were placed on constant readiness. Once the call came from brigade headquarters, the unit would be mobilised with weapons and sometimes the tanks would bomb up. Married soldiers would be brought in from their quarters and eventually the whole 'train set' would deploy into the field. The brigade staff would arrive and inspect, and perhaps put the regiment to some tests, after which all returned to base and stood down. This sounds like an ideal way of testing operational readiness, but the truth was that each unit knew almost the exact time it would receive the callout. The married soldiers would sleep in camp instead of at home during the period when the call was expected. Weapons were already fitted into the tanks to speed reaction times and ensure the regiment got a good tick in the box. While it was always reported as a great administrative feat, *Exercise Quick Train* proved nothing. *Quick Train* should have been called on Christmas Day to test the system (and thankfully it never was).

The 1970s were also marked by the RAC's intensive participation in *Operation Banner*, which marked its ability to deploy at full strength from 1969 through the following three decades.[47] The RAC's role in Northern Ireland was as armoured reconnaissance based on wheeled AFV squadrons or as extemporised infantry in urban and rural areas. In the first half of the 1970s, the RAC's helicopter resources backed up the light armoured vehicles and infantry. During the

Royal Armoured Corps Order of Battle, June 1972

Regiment June 1972	Garrison	Brigade	Abbreviation
The Life Guards	Detmold	20th Armoured Bde	LG
The Blues and Royals (Royal Horse Guards and 1st Dragoons)	A Sqn Aldergrove NI, Windsor	16th Airborne Bde	B&R
1st The Queen's Dragoon Guards	Catterick, Training Regiment RAC	UK Reserve	1QDG
The Royal Scots Dragoon Guards (Carabiniers and Greys)	Herford/ Edinburgh	I Corps Recce Regt	SCOTS DG
4th/7th Royal Dragoon Guards	Northern Ireland/Sennelager	6th Armoured Bde	4/7 RDG
5th Royal Inniskilling Dragoon Guards	Munster	4th Guards Bde	5 INNIS DG
The Queen's Own Hussars	Hohne	7th Armoured Bde	QOH
The Queen's Royal Irish Hussars	Paderborn	6th Armoured Bde	QRIH
9th/12th Royal Lancers (Prince of Wales's)	Detmold	20th Armoured Bde	9/12L
16/5th Queen's Royal Lancers	Omagh, Northern Ireland	UK Reserve	16/5L
17th/21st Lancers	A Sqn Northern Ireland, Sennelager	20th Armoured Bde	17/21L
The Royal Hussars	Tidworth (MBT), B Squadron Cyprus	5th Infantry Bde	RH
13th/18th Royal Hussars (Queen Mary's Own)	Bovington, Lulworth, Warminster; RAC Centre Regt	5th Infantry Bde	13/18H
14th/20th Kings Hussars	Hong Kong, Singapore, Tidworth, A Sqn NI	5th Infantry Bde	14/20H
15th/19th The King's Royal Hussars	Fallingbostel	11th Infantry Bde	15/19H
1st Royal Tank Regiment	Osnabruck	12th Mech Bde	1RTR
2nd Royal Tank Regiment	Bovington, Lulworth, Warminster; RAC Centre Regt	UK Reserve	2RTR
3rd Royal Tank Regiment	Wolfenbuttel	I Corps Recce Regt	3RTR
4th Royal Tank Regiment	Hohne and BATUS	7th Armoured Bde	4RTR
A Sqn QDG	Berlin	Berlin Field Force	

Saladin Armoured car of the SCOTS DG at Gosford Castle in 1972. Very little in the way of modification was carried out apart from the sections of makrolon on the turret, and the wire cutter forward of the turret. (R. Griffin)

One of the reverse flow Saracens bought back from abroad for use in Northern Ireland. The reverse flow cooling system is indicated by the raised rear louvres and the sheet metal cover at the front. This system was designed to help cooling in hot climates. One amusing aside was that due to the urgency of the requirement for these vehicles in Ulster, no effort was made to repaint them… so they were left in sand paint. At first this caused some worries from the local troublemakers because it made them very visible next to regular Saracens and they were singled out for attention, but eventually *everybody* got used to them… and then they were repainted. (R. Griffin)

The RAC in Northern Ireland, including Operation Banner 1959–1990

Regiment	1st Tour	2nd Tour	3rd Tour	4th Tour	5th Tour	6th Tour	7th Tour	8th Tour	9th Tour	10th Tour	11th Tour
15th/19th King's Royal Hussars	Aug 57–May 59	Aug 71	Nov 74–May 76	Jul–Nov 78 (detached Troops)	Sep–Dec 78 (detached Troops)	Mar–Jul 79 (detached Troop)	May–Jul 84 (A Sqn)				
11th Hussars (Prince Albert's Own)	Aug 59–Oct 60	disbanded 1969									
9th/12th Royal Lancers (Prince of Wales's)	Oct 60–Sep 62	Sep 72–Jan 73 (C Sqn)	May–Sep 73 (B Sqn)	Jan–May 75	May 76–Nov 77	Jul–Sep 82 (C Sqn)					
2nd Royal Tank Regiment	Sep 62–Dec 64 (less Cyclops)	Sep 73–Jan 74 (Badger)	Jan–May 74 (Ajax)	May–Sep 75 (Less Badger)	Aug–Dec 77 (Less Cyclops)	May 79–Nov 80	Feb–May 83 (Ajax)	Feb–May 89 (Huntsman)			
1st Queen's Dragoon Guards	Dec 64–Sep 66	Feb–May 74	Jan–May 76	Oct 78–Feb 79 (det Troop A Sqn)	Nov 78–Jan 79 (det Troop A Sqn)	May–Sep 79 (det Troop A Sqn)	Nov 79–Mar 80 (Detached Troop A Sqn)	Nov 80–Nov 82	May–Jul 89 (A Sqn)		
4th/7th Royal Dragoon Guards	Sep 66–Mar 69	May–Sep 72	Dec 74–Apr 75 (Recce Sqn)	Apr–Aug 76	Dec 77–Feb 78 (A Sqn Op. Bravado)	Dec 84–Feb 85	Jun–Aug 87 (D Sqn)				
17th/21st Lancers	Mar 68–Nov 71	Oct 71–Feb 73 (A Sqn)	Feb–Jun 73 (B Sqn)	Jun–Oct 73 (C Sqn)	Aug–Dec 73 (Air Sqn)	Nov 75–Mar 76	Dec 82–Feb 83 (A Sqn)				
Life Guards	Aug–Nov 69 (B Sqn)	Jun–Sep 70 (C Sqn)	Jul–Sep 70 (HQ+B Sqn)	Aug 70–Sep 71	Jul–Dec 72 (with C Sqn 4/7RDG)	May–Sep 74	Dec 75–Apr 76 (B Sqn)	Apr–Sept 77 (B Sqn)	Sep 77–Jan 78 (A Sqn)	Jan–Apr 78 (C Sqn)	–
Parachute Squadron RAC	Nov 69–Apr 70	Mar–Apr 71	Aug–Nov 71	Mar–Jun 73	Aug–Dec 75	disbanded 1976					
Royal Scots Greys	Jul–Sep 70 (B Sqn)	Feb–Jun 71 (C Sqn)	disbanded 1971								

The RAC in Northern Ireland, including Operation Banner 1959–1990

Regiment	1st Tour	2nd Tour	3rd Tour	4th Tour	5th Tour	6th Tour	7th Tour	8th Tour	9th Tour	10th Tour	11th Tour
14th/20th King's Royal Hussars	Nov 70–Mar 71 (C Sqn)	Jun–Sep 71 (A Sqn)	Aug–Oct 71 (HQ+C Sqn)	Jul–Nov 72 (A Sqn)	Jul–Nov 72 (C Sqn)	Nov 72–Mar 73 (Air Sqn)	Oct 72–Feb 73 (B Sqn)	Feb–May 74 (A Sqn)	Jul–Nov 74 (Air Sqn)	Oct 78–Feb 79	Jul–Oct 90
Blues and Royals	Apr–Aug 71 (A Sqn)	Nov 71–Mar 72 (B Sqn)	Mar–Jun 72 (A Sqn)	Jul–Sep 72 (B Sqn)	Nov 73–Feb 74 (C Sqn)	Feb–Jun 74 (A Sqn)	Jun–Aug 74 (B Sqn)	Apr–Aug 75 (C Sqn)	Dec 76–Apr 77	Feb–Jun 79	
Royal Hussars	Apr–Jun 71	Sep–71	Nov 72–Mar 73 (A Sqn)	Aug–Dec 74	Jun–Oct 78	Jan–Apr 86 (C Sqn)					
Royal Scots Dragoon Guards	Jul–Aug 71 (D Sqn)	Jul–Oct 72 (B Sqn)	Jun–Oct 73 (D Sqn)	May–Oct 76	Sep–Nov 80						
4th Royal Tank Regiment	Jul–Dec 71 (B+D Sqn)	Apr–Jul 76	Feb–Jun 78	Jun–Aug 86							
16th/5th Queen's Royal Lancers	Nov 71–May 73	Jul 76–Nov 76	Mar–Jul 80								
Queen's Own Hussars	Jan–May 72 (A Sqn)	Feb–Apr 72 (HQ+A Sqn)	Jun–Oct 73	May–Sep 77	Jun–Oct 79	Jan–Mar 87 (A+D Sqns)					
1st Royal Tank regiment	Jan–May 72 (C+D Sqn)	May 73–Nov 74	Dec 75–Apr 76 (Air Sqn)	Apr–Aug 77 (Less A Sqn)	Feb–Jun 79 (detached Troop)	Jul–Nov 79 (detached Troop)	Jun–Sep 81 (A Sqn)	Jul–Sep 89 (C Sqn)			
13/18th Royal Hussars (Queen Mary's Own)	Jan–May 72	Sep 75–Jan 76	Nov 77–May 79	Sep–Nov 85 (B Sqn)							
3rd Royal Tank Regiment	Jan–May 73	Sep 74–Jan 75	Dec 76–Apr 77 (A Sqn)	Apr–Jul 82 (B Sqn)							
Queen's Royal Irish Hussars	Dec 83-Feb 84 (D Sqn)										
5th Royal Inniskilling Dragoon Guards	Apr–Aug 81	Jul–Oct 90									

An RAF Westland Wessex taking off on an Eagle VCP mission from RAF Aldergrove during the 1980s. RAC troops participated in Eagle patrols flown by Royal Air Force and Army Air Corps helicopters. Nearly every chopper type employed by the RAF and AAC was employed on this duty at some point. (*Bob Girling*)

From 1981, the RAC's Irish regiments (along with the Irish regiments in the other arms of service) took their first turn on the Northern Ireland tours. In the 1970s, jobs like nuclear escort or other support roles were assigned to the Queen's Royal Irish Hussars and the 5th Inniskilling Dragoon Guards in absence of other units deployed in Ulster. The first Irish RAC regiment to deploy on Operation Banner was the 5th Inniskilling Dragoon Guards and, in the 1980s, all Irish regiments served in Northern Ireland at one time or another. This photo shows riot training with the 5th Inniskilling Dragoon Guards in West Germany prior to an Operation Banner tour in 1983. (*Home Headquarters RDG*)

second half of the 1970s, the infantry role became increasingly important. In the last decade of the Cold War the RAC's regiments served most often as the guard force at the Maze prison at Long Kesh.

Training for Northern Ireland was realistic and often dangerous. Riot control training, training in operations in urban areas and even armoured car work could be very different from what troopers were used to as MBT crews.

'The only injury I received over both Northern Ireland tours with 3rd RTR was a rubber bullet in the face during training in West Germany. It knocked a couple of teeth out, leaving me with two black eyes and a nasty friction burn on my right cheek.' (Pete Dobson, 3rd RTR)

Base areas in the Ulster countryside could be like those established at Gosford Castle or at Lisdhu House, or in more permanent postings such as those at Lisanelly Barracks in Omagh. The armoured reconnaissance squadrons operated over large areas and had troops stationed near IRA controlled locales. At Lisdhu, accommodation was in portacabins. The original house

The famous "Tin City", located on the Sennelager training area, was a mockup of a Northern Irish town. Tin City came complete with pubs, phone boxes, wrecked cars and all the buildings you would find in a small town. To give it size many buildings were simply corrugated tin painted to look like houses – hence the name Tin City! (*R. Griffin*)

Armoured vehicles parked at Gosford Castle in 1972. Gosford Castle was an RAC base used by detachments from most RAC regiments assigned to Operation Banner (*R. Griffin*)

was used for the operations room, for eating meals and for the all-important 'choggy shop'.[48] Gosford Castle served in the early 1970s as a similar outpost controlling Markethill and it was garrisoned by a succession of armoured reconnaissance squadrons. As the Troubles dragged on, the infantry were stretched to the limit. Urban *Operation Banner* deployments in Belfast or Londonderry were also very hazardous and troops could never relax their guard. Because the difference in manpower between an infantry company and an armoured squadron was significant, regiments had to combine squadrons in order to put enough boots on the ground. An average four month tour was undertaken in single or two squadron strength, but the effect on armoured training for units stationed in West Germany was disruptive and it sapped a regiment's strength. Some units did as many as ten or more tours on *Operation Banner* during the Cold War, and men were killed and wounded in sniper attacks, bombings and by well concealed booby traps.

Training for Northern Ireland at Sennelager with the SCOTS DG with typical realism. Training hard cut losses and learning infantry combat in an urban environment was very different from tactical training with armoured vehicles on Soltau! (*J.K. Webster*)

A typical paramilitary road block with militants wearing the 'uniform' of the time and trying to look intimidating. This is a Protestant road block in the early 1970s. (*R. Griffin*)

It is worth mentioning one unique role that was undertaken by the 4th/7th Royal Dragoon Guards as firefighters during the Belfast firemen's strike. Soldiers were trained to operate the Army's venerable Bedford Green Goddess fire engines, and others assumed the infantry role to act as close cordon travelling in Humber Pig APCs. This stood as a bright spot in what was otherwise a dangerous, depressing and thankless job trying to keep the peace as best as possible. *Operation Banner* went on through the rest of the Cold War. It complicated many regiments' Chieftain conversion – and it weakened BAOR in available units throughout the first half of the 1970s. Besides the men killed and wounded, service in Northern Ireland left psychological scars on hundreds of soldiers.

Much else changed in the armoured regiments of the 1970s, with the arrival of the CVR(T) for the Reconnaissance Troop, and the creation of the regimental Air Troop.[49] The Stalwart high mobility load carrier revolutionised the motor transport troop's job on the battlefield. Anti-Tank Guided Weapons (usually abbreviated to ATGW, and shortened to GW in the Royal Armoured Corps) were introduced into the order of battle.

Guided Weapons led a mixed life in the Royal Armoured Corps. The RAC did not embrace missiles as quickly as the infantry, to whom the Vigilant had been introduced in the early 1960s. The RAC's exposure to the missile came in its 1962 return to the airborne role it had experimented with during the latter part of the war. At first with the Parachute Squadron, 2nd Royal Tank Regiment and later as the RAC Parachute Squadron, the missile duly made its mark. The parachute squadron was equipped with the Malkara missile on the Humber Hornet

Another aspect of the Northern Ireland tours was Operation Bravado, providing support during the Firemen's strike. Crews from all three services were equipped with the venerable Green Goddess tenders. Sometimes the IRA fire brigade turned up at the same fires in Belfast – usually equipped with primitive stirrup pumps. (*R. Griffin*)

The Goddess was based on the Bedford RL truck and its distinctive nose can clearly be seen here. The author achieved one childhood dream though, driving through a busy city ringing the bell, no two tone sirens! To aid the Goddess' progress they were usually preceded by military police using their "blues and twos". (*R. Griffin*)

Here an ATO is about to deploy 'wheelbarrow' to check a suspicious vehicle. It was carried on a tray on a range of vehicles mounted, in this case, on the front of a Humber Pig APC. (*R. Griffin*)

This was one of the biggest fires that the 4th/7th RDG attended during their assignment to Operation Bravado; it raged for two days and the Goddesses were refilled while running. Visible in the picture is a ground mounted monitor which allowed a hose to be directed at the fire with no crew holding it because the pumps on the Goddess were extremely powerful and holding the hose was very tiring. (R. Griffin)

The infantry's Saxon was introduced into Northern Ireland in the 1980s to replace the older Humber Pig and Alvis Saracen. The RAC employed the Landrover Snatch in later deployments. (R. Griffin)

Soldiers of the 5th Inniskilling Dragoon Guards in the uniform and equipment introduced in the mid-1980s and carrying SA80 automatic rifles patrolling in Londonderry in 1989. (*Home Headquarters RDG*)

A patrol from the 5th Inniskilling Dragoon Guards standing behind a Landrover Snatch in Northern Ireland in 1989. The Northern Ireland situation continued for nearly a decade after the end of the Cold War. (*Home Headquarters RDG*)

Men of the 2nd RTR Parachute Squadron leap from a Blackburn Beverley in 1964. (*Dorian Llewellyn*)

This Humber Hornet is possibly a write off after a hard landing upside down. Fortunately nobody was injured. (*Dorian Llewellyn*)

Two Humber Hornets and a squadron lorry in a camp in Libya in 1964 – the 2nd Royal Tank Regiment then manned a permanent parachute squadron but the task was later assigned on a rotating basis within the RAC. (*Dorian Llewellyn*)

As always the pre-jump routine of checking and checking again was followed by the 2nd RTR Squadron's personnel. (*Dorian Llewellyn*)

A rear view of a preserved Humber Hornet. With a crew of two (driver and missile operator) two Malkaras could be fired with another two carried as a reload. (MR)

The big drawback of the Malkara was its slow flight and the Hornet's disadvantage was its poor cross-country performance. It did, however, provide airborne troops with a useful antitank capability until replaced by the Ferret Mk.5 which, like the Hornet, could be parachuted onto a battlefield. (MR)

launcher vehicle, carrying a crew of two and armed with four missiles. The Ferret Mk.2/6 armed with Vigilant was used in the independent armoured reconnaissance squadrons with Ferret Mk.2s employing one missile car per troop. An attempt at a more practical weapon followed in the Ferret Mk.5, a Ferret Mk.4 hull with a flat turret with a 7.62mm General Purpose Machine Gun in the centre flanked by twin Swingfire missile launchers on each side. The Swingfire could engage out to a range of 4000m and it was considered a very potent weapon. Only thirty-two Ferret Mk.5s were built so their numbers in armoured reconnaissance regiments were insignificant and even these were withdrawn at the end of 1977, to be replaced by the CVR(T) Striker.[50]

The Ferret Mk.5 earned its moment of glory before premature retirement in 1977. The RAC had troops on standby based at Tidworth throughout the 1960s and 1970s, including the Independent Armoured Car Squadron RAC, which could be deployed by air at short notice. The squadron was established on a rotating basis, and roughly consisted of a squadron of Ferret Mk.2 scout cars, but a troop of Mk.5s had joined the order of battle in the early 1970s. The 4th/7th Dragoon Guards were holding the role in 1974, when they suddenly received orders to depart for Cyprus after the Turkish Army had invaded the north of the island. Upon

The successor to the 2nd RTR's Parachute Squadron was the RAC Parachute Squadron, manned by detachments from different RAC regiments. Here members of the 16th/5th Lancers parachute Squadron are with a Ferret Mk.5 parked between two FV438s. The Ferret Mk.5 replaced the Hornet Malkara around 1970. (*The Lancer's Dropbox Media Group*)

Royal Armoured Corps Peacekeeping deployments in Cyprus and Lebanon 1960-1990

Cyprus UN Deployments 1960–1990 (includes Lebanon)

Unit	Deployments
Royal Horse Guards (The Blues)	Jan 60–Apr 60
14th/20th King's Hussars	Dec 62–Dec 66 (det sqns); Jan 73–May 73 (C Sqn)
1st The Royal Dragoons	Feb 64–Apr 64; Sep 75–Mar 76
Life Guards	Mar 64–Aug 64 (less B Sqn); Aug 64–Nov 64 (B Sqn); Mar 76–Sep 76 (A Sqn); Mar 79–Sep 79 (B Sqn); Jan 84–Jul 84 (C Sqn); Jan 86–Jul 86 (B Sqn); Jan 88–Jul 88 (A Sqn); Jan 89–Jul 89 (C Sqn)
2nd Royal Tank Regiment	Dec 64–May 65
5th Royal Inniskilling Dragoon Guards	Dec 65–Nov 67 (A Sqn); Oct 73–May 74
4th/7th Royal Dragoon Guards	Dec 67–Jun 68 (B Sqn); Jun 68–Dec 68 (C Sqn); Dec 73–Jun 74 (B Sqn)
3rd Royal Tank Regiment	Dec 68–Jun 69 (C Sqn); Sep 77–Mar 78 (C Sqn); Sep 78–Mar 79 (B Sqn); Apr 86–Apr 88 (F Sqn); Jun 88–Dec 88
Queen's Own Hussars	Jun 69–Dec 69 (B Sqn)
Royal Scots Greys	Dec 69–Jun 70 (B Sqn); Jun 70–Dec 70 (C Sqn)
Royal Hussars (Prince of Wales's Own)	Dec 70–Jun 71 (C Sqn); Jun 71–Dec 71 (A Sqn); Dec 71–Jun 72 (B Sqn)
Royal Scots Dragoon Guards	Jun 72–Dec 72 (D Sqn); Jan 75–Dec 75
Blues and Royals	Dec 72–Jun 73 (B Sqn); Sep 80–Mar 81 (C Sqn); Feb 82–Jul 82 (A Sqn); Jul 82–Jan 83 (B Sqn)
16th/5th The Queen's Royal Lancers	May 73–Dec 73 (A + B Sqns); Jul 74–Sep 74 (HQ+A Sqns); Dec 83–Mar 84 (A Sqn); Jan 85–Jul 85 (A Sqn)
Parachute Squadron Royal Armoured Corps	Jun 74–Oct 74
Queen's Royal Irish Hussars	Sep 74–Mar 75 (Less A+D Sqns); Sep 79–Mar 80 (B Sqn); Mar 81–Sep 81 (A Sqn)
1st Royal Tank Regiment	Apr 75–Oct 75
15th/19th The King's Royal Hussars	Jun 76–Nov 77 (C Sqn); Sep 76–Mar 77 (B Sqn); Mar 77–Sep 77 (A Sqn); Jun 88–Dec 88 (G Sqn)
9th/12th Royal Lancers (Prince of Wales's)	Nov 77–May 79 (C Sqn); Mar 78–Sep 78 (A Sqn); Jul 87–Jan 88 (A Sqn); Jul 88–Jan 89 (D Sqn)
13th/18th Royal Hussars (Queens Mary's Own)	May 79–Feb 81 (A Sqn); Mar 80–Sep 80 (B Sqn); Feb 81–Nov 82 (C Sqn); Sep 81–Feb 82 (B Sqn); Jan 87–Jul 87 (A Sqn)
1st Queen's Dragoon Guards	Jan 83–Jul 83 (C Sqn); Feb 83–Aug 83 (C Sqn); Aug 83–Dec 83 (A Sqn); Jul 85–Jan 86 (B Sqn); Jul 86–Jan 87 (D Sqn)
4th Royal Tank Regiment	Jul 83–Jan 84 (B Sqn); Jul 89–Jan 90 (B Sqn)
Lebanon	Jun 89–Jan 90

Crews from the 4th/7th Royal Dragoon Guards in Cyprus in 1974. The UN markings are very distinctive. (*R. Griffin*)

arrival, they became part of the United Nations force, and the little Ferret Mk.5s were put to good use. By their presence and with a great deal of bluff, the Turks were persuaded to keep off Nicosia International Airport. An amusing by-line to this deployment was that during a London street-lining parade rehearsal by the rest of the regiment the RSM had finally calculated all his distances. The regiment came on parade only for the RSM to find a large gap where the Independent Squadron should have been! Legend has it that somehow someone neglected to tell him they had left.

The most common Swingfire launcher was the tracked FV438 issued in the late 1960s to the Guided Weapons Troop in each armoured regiment. The Swingfire missile launcher was mounted on the hull roof and the FV438 had the added advantage of being reloadable under armour. This was a practical feature for a weapon system designed to fight in an NBC environment. The FV438 and the Swingfire were embraced and their potential and training was taken very seriously. The GW Troops achieved consistently high scores on the firing ranges. In late 1977 the Swingfire system was taken from the RAC and given to the Royal Artillery as a brigade level weapon. The rationale was that the Swingfire launchers could be grouped as a brigade asset under the Royal Artillery to provide long range anti-tank cover to the flanks of a battle group.

The size of Swingfire missiles only allowed the launch vehicles to carry a small number of reloads. Replenishments could only reach the front line in vulnerable Bedford trucks or loaded in Stalwarts. Sadly the Ministry of Defence did not adopt the FV431 load carrier which would have given more protection in such circumstances. Perhaps the most important beneficiaries

A view of the top surfaces of a white 4th/7th Royal Dragoon Guards Ferret Mk.2 in Cyprus in 1974. (*R. Griffin*)

Dalbeatty, an FV438 of the 4th Royal Tank Regiment's Guided Weapons Troop photographed at Tidworth in 1984. The Guided Weapons Troop was reinstated to the armoured and armoured reconnaissance regiments in 1984 after a seven year hiatus during which the Royal Artillery operated the Swingfire launchers in eight vehicle batteries. (*Keith Paget*)

Viewed from the left side, *Dalbeatty* has obviously received a number of Chieftain stowage bins to increase its external stowage, a practice that extended widely on RAC vehicles in the 1980s and continued on the Challengers deployed in Operation Granby in 1991. When the 4th RTR were the UK armoured regiment, B Squadron was deployed to the United Nations Peacekeeping Force in Cyprus for six months during the second half of 1983. (*Keith Paget*)

Red tops assisting an FV438 crew on the prairie. Getting lost was a real risk at BATUS and occurred regularly. Like the rest of the regiment the Guided Weapons Troop normally participated in the rotations into battlegroup training at BATUS. (*Richard Allen*)

An FV438 fires a Swingfire missile at snowy BATUS in the mid-1980s. (*Richard Allen*)

of the GW launcher's reintroduction into the RAC were the medium reconnaissance squadrons assigned as BAOR's divisional reconnaissance troops. The missiles returned to the Royal Armoured Corps in 1984 and resumed service much as they had originally been organized in the late 1960s. In the little Striker the new armoured reconnaissance regiments gained an all-terrain antitank capability lacking in the old armoured car regiment. There were many sensible reasons for the return of the Guided Weapons to the armoured regiments but, to the men of the GW Troops, it was simply a case of being better with missiles than artillerymen!

The RAC depended on many supporting arms, but the Royal Electrical and Mechanical Engineers (REME) were valued members of any armoured regiment's organization. After the war the Forward Repair Team (FRT) became the basic REME unit in RAC's armoured regiments. The techniques of tank recovery were practised and refined throughout the late 1940s but the introduction of newer tank designs like the Centurion did not generate any far-sighted solutions to how REME would be equipped. The Lend-Lease White and International Harvester Halftracks of American origin were kept in service as fitters' vehicles, and this role continued until the early 1970s. The range of special purpose tracked recovery vehicles so common in armoured formations in 1945 were eventually retired or scrapped and most RAC regiments by 1950 had a single type in service: the Churchill ARV Mk.2.

One of the first hard lessons learnt in Korea was the need for a Centurion based Armoured Recovery Vehicle (ARV). In the words of the 8th KRIH's commanding officer (written to the Director Royal Armoured Corps within a month of arrival in Korea) the Churchill ARV 'could not pull the skin off a banana'. The Centurion ARV Mk.1 was hurriedly converted from the Centurion

Detmold, West Germany, in 1964. This is the Squadron LAD Centurion Armoured Recovery Vehicle Mk.2 for B Squadron 3rd Carabiniers. (J. Dawson)

A Centurion of the 3rd Carabiniers under tow on Salisbury Plain training area in 1960. (*Barrie Dady*)

A Chieftain ARV at MVEE with the Atlas crane fitted. When the Challenger was introduced, the FV434 could no longer perform power pack changes due to the size of the CV12 engine. Fitting the Chieftain ARV with an Atlas crane was the answer. (*Brian Clarke*)

Mk.1 gun tank fleet, and the ARV Mk.2 was purpose built on the Vickers assembly lines. The Centurion ARVs were capable vehicles which served for many years. In the early days they were in relatively short supply and priority was naturally given to armoured regiments in BAOR. Centurion 'tugs' converted from gun tanks were used in the UK into the early 1960s because priority was given to producing Centurion gun tanks. In competent hands the Centurion ARV Mk.2 could recover a Conqueror, and it was issued on a scale of one ARV per sabre squadron. Between 1956 and 1966 a single Conqueror ARV (either an FV219 or FV222 – depending on availability) was issued to each regiment for the Headquarters Squadron Light Aid Detachment, for recovering Conquerors of any sabre squadron.

A Centurion gearbox being hoisted out of a Mk.8 Centurion at the Kuwaiti Army barracks, in Kuwait City. After C Squadron was deployed to Aden in 1960, the 3rd Carabiniers' A, B and HQ squadrons were sent to Kuwait to deter an Iraqi invasion in 1961. Lance Corporal Ken Standen of the 3rd Carabiniers A Squadron REME LAD is guiding the assembly out. (Barrie Dady)

The other end of the winch rope – Corporal B. Egleton of HQ Squadron operating the Scammel Explorer's winch gear in Kuwait 1961. (*Barrie Dady*)

A Chieftain of the 5th Inniskilling Dragoon Guards undergoing a pack lift in 1983. The Chieftain's reliability issues were addressed in the late 1970s and early 1980s by the Sundance programme which introduced many detail modifications and finally allowed the RAC's MBT a tolerable level of reliability. (*Home Headquarters RDG*)

A Fox CVR(W) of the Kent and Sharpshooters Yeomanry being serviced. As in other RAC regular regiments, attached REME personnel played key roles. (*Kent and Sharpshooters Yeomanry Museum*)

Changing a Centurion or Conqueror gearbox was simple, and was easily done in most conditions in two hours with a halftrack. The Centurion engine change was a major event because of the poor accessibility of key components. It took twelve hours in good conditions, but two days was common otherwise. This led to the power pack concept in the Chieftain design and to the development of vehicles like the FV434 fitters' vehicle which had a powered crane to perform pack lifts. A pack change on a Chieftain could be accomplished in two hours with a well-practiced crew – and practice was rapidly accumulated due to the terrible reliability record of the early Chieftains. When the Chieftain ARV was introduced it was modified to mount a powerful Atlas crane that could lift out power packs, which thereafter grew much heavier with the Challenger MBT.

The 1970s also brought a new North American training area into the RAC's experience. After the Gaddafi coup of 1969 in Libya, the British Army Training Unit Suffield (BATUS) was leased in 1971 for ten years from the Canadian government. Once the agreement was signed, much work followed in planning and building the base. Workshops, accommodations for visiting troops and permanent staff were all built. Facilities were primitive on the base but the small village of Rawlson around a mile from the base provided married quarters and a school for the base's children. In January 1972 BATUS was formally opened and in July the first rounds were fired by the first visiting battlegroup from the 4th Royal Tank Regiment under command of Lieutenant-Colonel Laurence New. The sheer size of the training area was a novelty to the men of the battlegroup.

At first training was limited to one squadron of MBTs and a company of mechanised infantry with supporting arms, including a battery of Abbot self-propelled guns. After the small training areas of West Germany the BATUS experience soon put much focus on smooth

In the mid-1960s, the 16th/5th Lancers took over the Reserve Regiment RAC role in Tidworth and deployed squadrons to Libya. These Centurion Mk.10s were photographed there in 1966 in an overall sand paint scheme. (*Geoffrey Wells*)

communications, strong map reading skills and developing tactical awareness at all levels. Training in Canada was enjoyed by most of the troops but was exhausting. The Chieftains were put to task far harder than in BAOR and worked better for it. The base eventually benefitted from better accommodations and went on to host nearly every conceivable mark of Chieftain, Ferrets, the whole FV430 and Warrior series, the whole CVR(T) family, and eventually the Challengers. BATUS had its lease extended in 1981, and again in 1991. In 2006 the Canadian government agreed that British forces could train at Suffield indefinitely.

As the base grew more established, exercises became more complex until BATUS ran full battlegroup training, using two squadrons of tanks and all supporting arms. The advantage of BATUS training was that it allowed troops to advance and engage targets with live fire. Training was realistic and could be very dangerous. The tanks fired live 120mm rounds to full effect and when technology moved on in the 1980s electronic simulation equipment came to the forefront. Range Safety Staff at BATUS held an important role in their Ferrets and other light AFVs with their upper surfaces painted red (affording them protection and ready identification). These 'redtops' had a critical job demanding constant vigilance of the battlegroup training. They served as umpires and kept exercise accidents to an absolute minimum.

Exercises known as Medicine Man 1–7 were held in BATUS from May to October each year. In later years four to six battlegroups underwent training on the Suffield base. Each battlegroup exercise lasted about twenty four days- and was supported by the BATUS staff and a dedicated 'enemy'. Traditionally the opposing forces were provided by a single nominated regiment for a given year. OPFOR duty at BATUS, like most things in the RAC, was a rotating appointment and was taken very seriously. BATUS training was a critical ingredient in the RAC's war making ability and drove the improvement of tactical doctrine and testing of new weapons under operational conditions.

In the 1960s the independent brigade group evolved into the 'square brigade' of two armoured regiments and two mechanised infantry regiments supported by an artillery regiment. In 1976 this changed when the British Army of the Rhine was reorganized into four armoured divisions based on two task forces each. The task forces had the same command

This is a famous or infamous BATUS incident (depending on which side of the fence you sit). Call sign Zero Charlie of the 4th/7th Royal Dragoon Guards broke down on the way back to Camp Crowfoot and was left there for what was meant to be a few days. Bad weather caused a delay in recovery and it was then found that frozen ground made the vehicle only recoverable using a small quantity of PE4 (the standard military explosive). As can be seen something did not go quite to plan and bits of Chieftain were hurled around the prairie, much to the amusement of some and to the horror of others! The tank was returned to the UK and underwent a complete refit before returning to the front line. (*R. Griffin*)

Freezing weather was common for BATUS after November. These were the conditions at Suffield in 1982 during *Medicine Man 6* with the 3rd Royal Tank Regiment. (*Rob Jacobs*)

BATUS staff kept the whole training unit together and always employed high visibility vehicles to ensure that they could be seen in a live weapons environment. (*Richard Allen*)

A battlegroup of the 5th Royal Inniskilling Dragoon Guards at BATUS in the middle of the 1980s on the Alberta prairie. (*Noel McLeery*)

A firing camp conducted by the 5th Inniskilling Dragoon Guards in 1984 on the Hohne ranges. Every regiment took its turn on the ranges, which were used by all of NORTHAG by the 1980s. The amount of room available on such a high demand training area, and accessibility amidst the demands of multiple units, compared very poorly with what Suffield had to offer. (*Home Headquarters RDG*)

The snow background shows up the garish BATUS staff Ferret Mk.1 to advantage. (*Richard Allen*)

A Chieftain Mk.10 bogged at BATUS in August 1989. (*Rob Jacobs*)

A Chieftain Mk.10 minus its skirting plates moving across the Alberta prairie at Suffield in the late 1980s. (*R. Griffin*)

Medicine Man 5 in 1989 was the scene of this dust cloud caused by dry conditions and the movement of a battlegroup across the grassland. A Chieftain and the Recce Troop CVR(T)s of the 3rd RTR can be seen with conspicuous markings. (*Rob Jacobs*)

An atmospheric view of a Chieftain and a range control Ferret at dawn at BATUS in the 1980s. (*Richard Allen*)

At BATUS the Chieftains took a hell of a beating and this 3rd RTR example seen in 1989 needs its suspension examined at the end of a hard day's work. (*Rob Jacobs*)

A happy and exhausted Chieftain Mk.10 crew at BATUS in 1989. This tank has lost its right side front stowage bins and part of its track guards. The tracks have lost their rubber pads and are polished from the sandy soil. (*Rob Jacobs*)

The mighty Challenger 1 made its appearance with the 5th Inniskilling Dragoon Guards just prior to its amalgamation with the 4th/7th Royal Dragoon Guards as The Royal Dragoons in 1992. This one was photographed cresting a rise with gun depressed in the early 1990s. Combined with high tech simulation equipment and training aids, BATUS battlegroup training prepared RAC crews for war very effectively. (*Home Headquarters RDG*)

The prairie at Suffield was not all well drained level ground and the topography of the base held plenty of surprises. Here a Chieftain of the 5th Inniskilling Dragoon Guards is bogged and waiting for recovery in 1983. (*Home Headquarters RDG*)

The BATUS training area required large call sign markings and radio zapcodes for staff umpiring and battle group control. (*Home Headquarters RDG*)

structure as mechanized or armoured brigades. The artillery, infantry and logistic field forces allotted to each division could be augmented as needed by the 1st British Corps headquarters. The mobility of the mechanised infantry in the task forces was improved by the adoption of the FV432 APC, which could follow the main battle tanks better than the wheeled Saracen. The reality of this new order of battle was that much of BAOR's infantry was deployed in Northern Ireland or was based in the United Kingdom. In time of war everything would have depended on quick reinforcement.

Armoured regiments underwent a few changes between the middle of the 1970s and the end of the Cold War. The arrival of the Chieftain and the amalgamations of 1969–1971 resulted briefly in maintaining smaller armoured regiments of forty- three MBTs (three squadrons of fourteen tanks with a single tank in RHQ). The changes were normally visible in the number of tanks available to squadron and regimental headquarters troops and this enabled more regiments to convert quickly to the Chieftain. The arrival of the Scorpion and Scimitar to replace the Ferrets in the reconnaissance troops, the disappearance of the regimental air troop and the provision of a Guided Weapons Troop were also changes that endured until the 1990s. The Chieftain had all the advantages one could have asked for in a defensive battle (excepting mechanical reliability for its first decade and a half in service). On the basis of the fourteen tank squadron, the Type 57 regiment with four squadrons became the most common type of Chieftain regiment in BAOR in the 1980s. The loss of the air troops by the late 1970s was a blow to many commanders, especially those who could remember the flexibility gained from reconnaissance performed by trained AFV crewmen since the campaign in Malaya. The air troops were withdrawn against the recommendations of senior RAC officers. The economic reality of keeping helicopter assets concentrated in the Army Air Corps negated the strong tactical benefits that armoured regiments had gained from being able to conduct their own reconnaissance flights.

A Chieftain Mk.5 of the 3rd RTR's B Squadron No.5 Troop in 1980. This vehicle still has the .50 ranging gun which remained part of the Chieftain's equipment until the Tank Laser Sight (introduced in the mid-1970s) was deemed reliable enough to supplant it in the 1980s. (*Dick Taylor*)

A Royal Scots Dragoon Guards (or SCOTS DG) Chieftain crossing open ground during Troop Training on Soltau, West Germany in the early 1980s. (*J.K. Webster*)

The introduction of Simfire and similar battlefield simulator devices made combat training more realistic in the late 1970s and early 1980s. This is a SCOTS DG Chieftain 'brewed up' in training in 1984. (*J.K. Webster*)

A Chieftain of the SCOTS DG crossing the Soltau training ground at speed during brigade training in 1983. (*J.K. Webster*)

The Queen's Parade at Sennelager in 1985. In the 3rd RTR, as almost every other armoured regiment, no two Chieftains were painted quite the same! (*Rob Jacobs*)

A Chieftain Mk.10, with simulator equipment fitted, on exercise in BAOR in the late 1980s. (*R. Griffin*)

An NBC exercise in BAOR in the 1980s. This would have been a headquarters section with a bridgelayer, LAD detachment and a Chieftain Mk.9 leading. (*R. Griffin*)

Fitted with a SIMFIRE fire simulator, a 5th Inniskilling Dragoon Guards Chieftain Mk.10 commanded by Lieutenant Jackson splashes through a mud puddle on the Soltau training area in 1986. (*Home Headquarters RDG*)

The Mk.10 was fitted with Stillbrew turret appliqué armour and additional armour around the turret ring. (*Home Headquarters RDG*)

Crews had to be able, under any conditions, to recover a breakdown if the squadron ARV was indisposed or knocked out. Here we can see troop level recovery training in 1983 on the Soltau training area. The two Chieftains are from the 5th Inniskilling Dragoon Guards. (*Home Headquarters RDG*)

When the Chieftains' .50 inch ranging gun was removed, as earlier vehicles were rebuilt to Mk.8 and Mk.9 standard, the mounting aperture was plugged, welded, and ground smooth. This 1993 photo shows a line of Chieftains of the 5th Inniskilling Dragoon Guards waiting to drive onto railway flats before moving to a training area. (*Home Headquarters RDG*)

A spectacular night-time shoot with 120mm guns photographed during a SCOTS DG gunnery camp in the early 1980s. The Chieftain relied on infrared and image intensification devices for night driving and gunnery up until the last years of the Cold War, when the Mk.11 introduced a TOGS thermal gunnery system derived from that fitted to the Challenger 1. (*J.K. Webster*)

Chapter Eleven

The 1980s and the End of the Cold War

The early 1980s held surprises for the Royal Armoured Corps. The Falklands are not ideal tank country, but the RAC deployed the CVRT family during *Operation Corporate* in 1982. With a ground pressure less than that exerted by the average soldier, they proved ideal support vehicles. Two troops from the Blues and Royals were deployed, consisting of four Scorpions and four Scimitars armed with the RARDEN 30mm cannon. This weapon was extremely accurate and could have easily dealt with any armoured vehicle deployed by the Argentinians. A Samson recovery vehicle was also deployed, crewed by a REME detachment. The CVR(T)s were able to drive over most of the Falkland boggy ground with no problems and they provided fire support in several engagements, losing one Scorpion damaged by a mine.

D Squadron, The Queen's Own Hussars served as the Berlin Squadron in 1983. Visible are a Chieftain Mk.5 still fitted with the .5 in ranging gun, a Ferret Mk.2 and an FV432 APC – all wearing the new Berlin urban scheme. (J. Steadman)

By the 1980s the addition of wire mesh stowage trays over the engine became common on Ferrets. This vehicle belonged to D Squadron, QOH in 1983. (*J. Steadman*)

The Berlin Squadron had some sixteen Chieftains, one of which is seen here on the ranges flying a green flag to denote that all guns are unloaded. (*J. Steadman*)

A fine study of a Chieftain of D Squadron QOH in 1983, showing the intricacies of the Berlin scheme which was designed to break up the vehicle's silhouette against the brick and mortar of an urban battlefield. (*J. Steadman*)

D Squadron QOH manned the Berlin Squadron from April 1983 until April 1985. The previous tenants of Smuts Barracks, West Berlin had been D Squadron 4th/7th RDG – the first to use the Berlin scheme. (*J. Steadman*)

Rear view of a QOH Chieftain in Berlin. The Chieftain was known for its clouds of white exhaust smoke. (*J. Steadman*)

In the early 1980s the 1st British Corps' organization changed again; the 1st and 3rd Armoured Divisions (supported by part of the 4th Armoured Division) remained in West Germany. The 2nd Infantry Division returned to the United Kingdom. The Berlin Field Force was renamed the Berlin Brigade in 1983 and continued to operate outside the BAOR command chain. The BAOR divisions were now composed of armoured and mechanized task forces (which were created on the basis of the familiar brigades) reinforced by field forces of infantry and supporting arms as situations required. This arrangement continued until the end of the Cold War on the assumption that in action the available supporting artillery, engineers and infantry reinforcements would be parcelled out to support self-sufficient battlegroups. These were the tactics practised so hard at BATUS with the goal of inter-arms cooperation and flexibility. The result of the tactical evolution of the battlegroup system was finally tested out against Saddam Hussein's Army in February 1991 with great success.

A Challenger 1 at the Longcross test track at Chobham in Surrey. The Military Vehicle Experimental Establishment (MVEE) tested all Britain's tank designs and was the heir of the FVRDE organization. (*Brian Clarke*)

The Challenger 1 was much more capable than the older Chieftain – but also larger and heavier and its crews had to adapt to a more complex vehicle. (*Brian Clarke*)

The advanced armour carried by the Challenger I, with its powerful engine and advanced suspension, made the tank one of the world's most powerful. The real drawback was that its fire control system was the same as the Chieftain's and a generation behind tanks like the Leopard 2 and Abrams. When the Challenger saw action in 1991 it proved more than up to the tasks of the modern battlefield. (*Brian Clarke*)

The Challenger's Chobham armour's long evolution came in many steps. In 1957–1958 spaced armour was tested extensively on a series of Conqueror and Centurion vehicles built specially for evaluation with 183mm HESH rounds and antitank missiles. These trials, which ran well into the 1960s, steered British designers away from spaced armour and towards more effective systems of passive armour protection. In the early 1960s the use of multilayer armour incorporating layers of ceramic and steel was pioneered at the research establishment at Chobham to defeat hollow charge and kinetic energy attack to become the starting point for the revolutionary protection system developed by the British and shared with their allies. The Challenger I and M1 Abrams were the first to carry this form of protection in a production main battle tank and further development continues today. (*Crown Copyright*)

The MVEE turned its efforts towards steel and ceramic laminated armour from about 1964 onwards resulting in the development of the Chobham armour introduced on the M1 Abrams and Challenger 1 in the early 1980s. Britain shared the technology with the United States and West Germany. (*Crown Copyright*)

The gun/armour race persisted after the Cold War. 02 SP 86 was originally 05 FA 86. The unusual turret configuration is a result of trials concerned with mounting a 140mm gun. As this would have been out of balance due to its size various methods were tested to find a solution using a modified L11 series gun mounting welded further forward. This Chieftain never returned to front line service and was finally scrapped in 2011. (*Brian Clarke*)

This Chieftain carries a SP (Special Projects) number indicating it is in use for trials. In this shot the gunners armoured hood has been removed; what appears to be some optical test kit is placed above it with the power lead just visible. Many trials like this took place to evaluate new equipment – with the details of most never seeing the light of day. This was the reality of the arms race throughout the Cold War. (*Duncan McKenzie*)

Like tactics and orders of battle, the tank also evolved in the last decade of the Cold War. The plan to replace the Chieftain with a more powerful battle tank was tabled almost from the moment it entered service. The element of protection was taken to its highest form in the Chobham armour perfected in 1969. The main problem was that the British Army could not afford to upgrade the Chieftain with Chobham armour and it had to wait for the introduction of the next generation of British Main Battle Tank in the 1980s. Projects were undertaken with the Federal Republic of Germany for a common MBT and also to build an all-British MBT named the MBT-80. Little more than a few experimental prototypes and paper studies occurred before the RAC determined to evolve a new tank from the Chieftain's best features. This approach was reinforced by the long years of teething problems experienced with the Chieftain's complex powerpack and dissatisfaction with its low power to weight ratio. In the decade after the Chieftain's introduction the development of improved sub-systems that functioned with Chieftain's proven gun and basic layout proceeded. The Challenger was to all intents a super Chieftain developed for Iran, with a new V12 diesel, a hydropneumatic suspension and with Chobham armour. It brought no huge improvements in fire control over late model Chieftains. Its design represented safe and sure steps – evolution and not

Seen on a snowy day in 1985, a Challenger Mk.2 throws up the frozen earth on a West German training area. The first regiment to receive the Challenger was The Royal Hussars in 1983, but the 17th/21st Lancers, Queen's Royal Irish Hussars, the SCOTS DG, the 14th/20th Hussars, the Life Guards, the 2nd Royal Tank Regiment and the 3rd Royal Tank Regiment all converted to the new MBT before the end of the Cold War. (*Bob Girling*)

Taken from the cockpit of an RAF Chinook in November 1985, this photo shows a battlegroup of Challenger tanks, mechanized infantry and M109 self-propelled howitzers. The Challenger MBT and Warrior MICV were faster and more flexible weapons than the Chieftain and FV432, but, due to economic factors, the two older designs remained in service after the Cold War. Fast, well protected, heavily armoured and maneuverable, the Challenger and Warrior were ideal partners in the battlegroup formations that, by the mid-1980s, formed the core tactical principle in BAOR. (*Bob Girling*)

revolution. Its fire control system received much criticism after the NATO Canadian Army Trophy tank gunnery competition of 1987, but it was a far more effective combat vehicle than the T-72 it might have faced. At sixty-two tons it was, with the American Abrams, the most heavily armoured MBT in the world.

The Challenger purchase at first merely included two hundred and forty new MBTs. This equipped only four armoured regiments, and the rest of the RAC had to continue with upgraded Chieftains. This created the problem that logistics in the field would have to cope with two types of spares, but became the reality for the Royal Armoured Corps who made it work. In late 1982 the Challenger was accepted by the general staff with several unresolved design issues. Because of these another year would elapse before it began to be issued, but more than 400 would eventually be ordered. The British armoured force in the last few years of the Cold War was composed of the new Challengers, about eight hundred Chieftains and the large CVR(T) family.

Conclusion

Previous works have pointed to the cavalry and the RTR as separate identities within the Royal Armoured Corps. During the Cold War, the Royal Armoured Corps succeeded in forging a corps identity, but no higher power has ever extinguished the cavalry's view of itself as distinct from the Royal Tank Regiment. As in most branches of the British Army, this tradition-bound sense of self identity has become a source of great strength and encompasses a very close attachment to armour. The RAC has only grown into a closer family of regiments since 1945, and most of the difference between cavalry and Royal Tank Regiment identities faded after the 1960s.

The Cold War ended unexpectedly in November 1989, but the army kept much of its forces as they were until 1992. *Options for Change* resulted in a large reduction of the Royal Armoured Corps who had spent the interim fighting a lightning war in Kuwait in early 1991. Operation Granby vindicated the RAC's tactical doctrines and training arrangements. The units remaining in Germany waited for the inevitable military reduction as the signs of Soviet collapse became more evident. In the years to come the RAC saw more amalgamations and many Cold War RAC soldiers opted to leave the army for civilian life. For the first decade of the post-Cold War era Britain had a strong economy and deployments in the Balkans kept those who stayed on busy. Even Northern Ireland eventually calmed after the 1998 Good Friday Agreement and BAOR became British Forces Germany, shrunk to a shadow of its former self. The world had changed.

The men who served in the RAC in the Cold War have cause to be proud of the roles they played in a tense and dangerous era. Loyalties to the regiments and to the comrades of days passed are still evident. Many veterans are still active in the regimental associations, and Facebook pages and Old Comrades Forums on the internet keep the memories alive. Some old soldiers have chosen to close the chapter on their army career, others have faithfully attended every reunion and outing of their regimental association for decades. A few have even maintained a relationship with armoured vehicles or with museums that show posterity the story of their regiments and their modern day descendants. Their service is remembered, and we hope that this book will encourage others to study all of these regiments and do their individual stories full justice.

The headquarters troop of The Royal Dragoon Guards, amalgamated from the 4th/7th Royal Dragoon Guards and the 5th Royal Inniskilling Dragoon Guards, seen in 1994. One of the hard realities of the end of the Cold War was that amalgamations again faced the Royal Armoured Corps. (*Home Headquarters RDG*)

The character of the British Army has changed much in the new century, with the long wars in Afghanistan and in Iraq. Unchanged is the loyalty that each soldier feels to his regiment, and the professionalism that has characterized the Royal Armoured Corps in past times and in the present. Fundamental to that professionalism, transcending rank and time, are the camaraderie and senses of duty and of shared responsibility. (*Home Headquarters RDG*)

Notes

1. One example amongst wartime regimental commanders who accepted a lesser rank to stay in the army after the war was Lieutenant-Colonel Eugene V. Strickland. Strickland had fought at Arras in 1940, received a commission and eventually commanded the North Irish Horse and 145th Regiment RAC in Tunisia and Italy in 1944. Strickland became a major again after the war and commanded a squadron of the 16th/5th Lancers on detachment from RAC headquarters. Strickland finished his career as a major-general. Many other officers who had similar levels of battle and command experience from wartime service stayed on in the RAC after the war as career officers. "*Python*" was the code name given for leave given to troops who had served overseas for over four years and who were due for home posting. It meant reassignment to duties in the UK, generally followed by discharge from the army.

2. See *The Scarlet and Green Journal* (regimental magazine of the 16th/5th Lancers) of 1946 and the *Feather and Carbine* of 1946 (regimental magazine of the 3rd Carabiniers). Both recount the disruption that followed the war in Europe and in India, listing departures of personnel, changes of base areas and the return of sports and educational pastimes in units waiting to return to the United Kingdom after years abroad. The 16th/5th Lancers were stationed in Italy at war's end but within a year they found themselves in North Africa. The experience was typical for many units.

3. See p.192. Macksey, Kenneth. *A History of the Royal Armoured Corps and its Predecessors 1914 to 1975.* Newtown Publications, Beaminster, England. 1983.

4. The army made the changes to the officer reserve public in regimental journals as well as by other channels. An explanation of the changes exists in the 1948 edition of *The Scarlet and Green Journal.*

5. See p.189 Forty, George. The Royal Tank Regiment, a Pictorial History 1916–2001. Second Edition. Halsgrave, England. 2001. The Royal Tank Regiment reactivated the 40th RTR, 41st RTR, 42nd RTR, 43rd RTR, 44th RTR, and 45th RTR as Territorial regiments, each of which had been a wartime regiment affiliated to a specific depot area and to a regular Royal Tank Regiment. In Scotland the Lothian and Border Horse Yeomanry served as a territorial regiment affiliated to the largely Scottish 4th Royal Tank Regiment. Two London based Yeomanry regiments, the Westminster Dragoons and the 3rd/4th County of London Yeomanry, were affiliated to the 2nd Royal Tank Regiment. In the cavalry, the county based yeomanry regiments fulfilled the same territorial functions and already had long standing ties to individual cavalry regiments. In general these regular and territorial regiments shared common recruiting areas and the system was well tried from the shared experience of the Second World War.

6. See p.194, Macksey.

7. See *The Feather and Carbine* 1947. This edition of the magazine describes barrack areas in Aldershot, Bordon and Perham Down in much the same manner. It was obviously a huge disappointment for troops coming home after years abroad and having fought the Burma campaign.

8. See p.423–424 Brereton, J.M. *A History of the 4th/7th Royal Dragoon Guards and their predecessors 1685–1980.* Published by the Regiment. Catterick. 1982.

9. See Griffin, Robert. *Conqueror.* The Crowood Press. England. 1999.

10. See p.196, Macksey. This is also explained in the author's *Conqueror* title.

11. In file WO216/429 in the National Archives, Kew, a note exists dated 23rd June 1952 addressed to the Prime Minister detailing the need to sell Centurions to Canada and the United States MAP in order to fund British Army Centurion requirements.

12. See p.200 Macksey and see p.24–20 'A History of the 1st British Corps', 1st British Corps Headquarters. Bielefeld, West Germany. 1967. This BAOR produced pamphlet has an excellent description of the corps' changing composition between reactivation and 1967, including detailed description of two corps exercises held by 1st British Corps in 1961 and 1967.

13. See p.4 Addyman, Ronald. *National Service in Libya in 1949 with the Armoured Regiment The 4th/7th Royal Dragoon Guards.* Published by the Author, Leeds 2012.

14. See p.11 Crosskill, Allan. *A Simple Soldier: Join the Army; Learn a Trade, Adventure, Travel & Get Paid.* Published by the Author, England. 2006. This same sequence of events joining up seems to have been universal (as was the surprise of many at the better accommodations in Germany) and was confirmed to the author in correspondence with former 3rd Carabiniers.

15. p.298 5th Royal Inniskilling Dragoon Guards Journal. 1954 Edition.

16. See Thompson, Ralph. The 15th/19th The King's Royal Hussars: a Pictorial History.

17. An excellent short and humorous account of joining up in 1955 can be found in Crosskill, Allan. *A Simple Soldier: Join the Army; Learn a Trade, Adventure, Travel & Get Paid.* Published by the author, England, 2006. The complete list of motives of a young man of seventeen joining the army can never be adequately enumerated, and some simply joined up for something to do.

18. p.191 Macksey. Major Kenneth Macksey served as a squadron commander in the 4th Royal Tank Regiment for many years after the war and became an eminent military historian. His book remains the most comprehensive history of the RAC available, treating for example the entire period of the Second World War up to 1975. His analysis of the RAC's internal dynamics was that the corps had grown into a closer family by the middle of the 1970s, a process that has advanced considerably since the end of the Cold War.

19. p.191–192 Ibid. Macksey's study of the RAC written in 1983 enumerated the internal divisions within the Royal Armoured Corps at the highest levels of its officer corps. These differences were far more obvious in the years immediately following the Second World War than in the decades that followed. Throughout the last chapters of Macksey's work it is plain to see that in his view amalgamations, the reduction in size of the corps and the common experiences of long deployments like Northern Ireland drove the two sides of the corps together during the Cold War, and ultimately brought something akin to unity.

20. See War Diary 8th Hussars December 1950 and January 1951, which includes the correspondence between Lieutenant-Colonel Jumbo Phillips and the DRAC (Major-General N.W. Duncan) as well as after action reports from the few survivors of Cooper Force describing prisoners being shot out of hand by the communist forces. Lieutenant-Colonel Sir W. Guy Lowther, (5th Baronet Lowther of Swillington) proved the Centurion design in combat in Korea, becoming the commanding officer of the 8th Hussars in 1951 and remaining so until 1954.

21. See 1st Royal Tank Regiment Korean Report for May 1953 in War Diary 1st Royal Tank Regiment May 1953.

22. See p.197 Macksey. The quoted figure of seven hundred reservists is an astonishing percentage of the 8th Hussars strength, and that was the number necessary to call up in order to mobilise the regiment for service in Korea.

23. See History of the 1st British Corps.

24. Many surviving documents criticise the Conqueror design for poor mobility and mechanical reliability. These include the section on p.428 of the Brereton History of the 4th/7th RDG and also at some length on p.34 in Crosskill.

25. See p.67 Regimental Journal of the 3rd Kings Own Hussars Volume V No.2 April 1956. Not all regiments received Conquerors at the same time despite the short production run. The 9th Lancers only got theirs in 1958, at the same time as their Ferrets.

26. See p.203 Macksey.

27. The army was completely unready for the deployment of an armoured force outside of BAOR, and the Royal Tank Regiment units' involvement had to be improvised. The 6th RTR learnt to wade and

the 7th RTR had to relearn wartime lessons on the old amphibious LVT-4 Buffalo and on LVT-3s. A thirty two man group from the 7th RTR under Captain Peter Berry formed No 1 Landing Vehicle Troop RAC, tasked with landing 40 RM Commando and 42 RM Commando, with a minimum of training. They landed at Port Said at 0415hrs on November 6th 1956; C Squadron 6th RTR waded ashore minutes later in their Centurions and was quickly reinforced by the rest of the regiment. The 1st RTR was left as a reserve on Malta for the duration of the crisis. See 4th RTR and 7th RTR History website (1953–1961 section) researched by Major-General Sir Laurence New, p.203 Macksey, and File WO32/17391 Suez (National Archives).

28. See History of the 1st British Corps.
29. p.178 Regimental Journal of the 3rd King's Own Hussars Volume V No 4. September 1958.
30. See History of the 1st British Corps and p.204–205 Macksey.
31. See History of the 1st British Corps and see p.161 Taylor, D. *Warpaint: Colours and Markings of British Army Vehicles 1903–2003 Volume 3*. Stratus, Poland. 2011.
32. See p.204–205 Macksey.
33. Originally three hundred and sixty Conquerors were to be ordered to equip Divisional Regiments RAC – essentially heavy gun tank regiments. The National Archive File WO216/429 of 1952 details this information as well as the intention to buy a number of 120mm Centurions (Conway) to serve with the normal 20-pounder armed tanks (in the same manner as the Sherman Firefly had in the war), along with a need for two thousand Centurions for British needs. The Conway was never procured and these orders for Conquerors were never made. When the FV214 entered service, they took on the role envisioned for the 120mm Centurions in normal armoured regiments.
34. See A History of the 1st British Corps.
35. With thanks to Mr Richard Allen, 9/12th Lancers.
36. See Feather and Carbine 1965.
37. *Gasthausen* aside, the dangers of manoeuvres in BAOR were very real and fatalities amongst units on exercise are well documented. The 3rd Carabiniers lost their RSM to a training ground accident in West Germany, and men were also lost training in Libya and in BATUS right up to the end of the Cold War.
38. See History 1st British Corps.
39. See Feather and Carbine 1961.
40. Detached troops of the 16th/5th Lancers' Centurions serving under the 4th RTR's command in the Radfan were the first to fire the L7 105mm gun in anger. The Scarlet and Green Journal 1964.
41. See Scarlet and Green Journal 1964.
42. See p.204–205 Macksey.
43. See p.193–194 Macksey.
44. See p.206 Macksey.
45. Studies of the Chieftain have been written by George Forty, and Simon Dunstan in the 1980s and more recently by Simon Dunstan and also by the author Rob Griffin. The Chieftain was adopted first by two cavalry regiments in 1966–1967, the 11th Hussars and 17/21st Lancers.
46. The CAT Trophy eluded British efforts for the rest of the Cold War.
47. See p.215 Forty, G. *The Royal Tank Regiment, a Pictorial History*. Operation Banner is described as other arms in the infantry role. Almost all RAC regiments did a tour in Northern Ireland, even the corps' two Irish regiments, the KRIH and the 5 INNIS DG, although only after the late 1970s.
48. This term would not of course be politically correct in modern parlance.
49. See p.209, Macksey and p.214, Forty. Armoured car regiments (and later on, armoured reconnaissance regiments) and armoured regiments all theoretically created air troops in the 1960s but these disappeared in the early 1970s. As useful as these proved for regimental reconnaissance capabilities, helicopters were judged to be more useful as Army Air Corps 'property' that could be better used attached to brigades or divisions.
50. Armoured Recovery Vehicle development had received little funding since the end of the war. Early reports from Korea were especially scathing about the Churchill ARV Mk.II, as can be seen in the War Diary 8th Hussars December 1950. The Centurion tugs used as extemporised ARVs in Korea are mentioned in the War Diary 1st Royal Tank Regiment for April-May 1953 although the Centurion ARV Mk.1 was then also available.

Appendix I

Territorial RAC Regiments 1947–1990

Territorial Army Regiment, RAC	Recruitment Area	Regular army affiliation	Years active (RAC role)	Notes
3rd/4th County of London Yeomanry (Sharpshooters)	London	2nd RTR, 1st The Royal Dragoons	1947–1961	amalgamated with Kent Yeomanry to form Kent and Shapshooters Yeomanry
Ayrshire Yeomanry	Scotland	Scots Greys	1947–1967	transferred RCT 1969
Cheshire Yeomanry	Cheshire	3rd Carabiniers, 5 INNIS DG after 1971	1947–1969	became part of Queen's Own Yeomanry
City of London Yeomanry (Rough Riders)	London	2nd RTR	1947–1956 (became infantry)	amalgamated with Inns of Court Regt 1961
Derbyshire Yeomanry	Derbyshire	12th Lancers	1947–1957	amalgamated with Leicestershire Yeomanry
Duke of Lancaster's Own Yeomanry	Lancashire	14th/20th Hussars	1947–1967	amalgamated with 40th/41st RTR
East Riding of Yorkshire Yeomanry	Yorkshire	3rd Carabiniers	1947–1956	amalgamated with Yorkshire Hussars Yeomanry and The Queen's Own Yorkshire Dragoons Yeomanry to form The Queen's Own Yorkshire Yeomanry
The Fife and Forfar Yeomanry	Scotland	1st The Royal Dragoons	1947–1969	amalgamated with the Scottish Horse to form The Fife and Forfar Yeomanry/Scottish Horse in 1956
The Queen's Own Royal Glasgow Yeomanry	Scotland	The Royal Scots Greys	1947–1956	amalgamated with Lanarkshire Yeomanry and 1/2nd Lothian and Border Horse to form The Queen's Own Lowland Yeomanry
Royal Gloucestershire Hussars	Gloucestershire	11th Hussars to 1969, The Royal Hussars thereafter	1947–1967	1967–1969 reconstituted as infantry then disbanded, raised from 1971 as part of Royal Wessex Yeomanry
The Inns of Court Regiment	London	The Life Guards, The Royal Horse Guards (The Blues)	1947–1961	Absorbed Northamptonshire Yeomanry 1956, amalgamated with The City of London Yeomanry (Rough Riders) as The Inns of Court and City Yeomanry (RAC) in 1961, disbanded in 1967 and subsequently raised as Royal Signals 1971–1975
The Lanarkshire Yeomanry	Scotland	The Royal Scots Greys	1947–1956	amalgamated with Queen's Own Royal Glasgow Yeomanry and 1st/2nd Lothians and Border Horse to form The Queen's Own Lowland Yeomanry.
The Leicestershire Yeomanry (Prince Albert's Own)	Leicestershire	7th Queen's Own Hussars	1947–1957	amalgamated with the Derbyshire Yeomanry to form the Leicestershire and Derbyshire Yeomanry in 1957.

Territorial Army Regiment, RAC	Recruitment Area	Regular army affiliation	Years active (RAC role)	Notes
1st/2nd Lothians and Border Horse	Scotland	4th RTR, thereafter SCOTS DG	1947–1956	amalgamated with Lanarkshire Yeomanry and The Queen's Own Glasgow Yeomanry to form The Queen's Own Lowland Yeomanry
The Northamptonshire Yeomanry	Northamptonshire	8th King's Royal Irish Hussars	1947–1961	converted to Royal Engineers
The North Irish Horse	Northern Ireland	1st The King's Dragoon Guards, 5th INNIS DG, QRIH	1947–1967	raised as D Squadron Royal Yeomanry Regiment after 1969
The North Somerset Yeomanry	Somerset	3rd Hussars	1947–1956	Airborne RAC TA element, amalgamated with 44th/50th RTR to form The North Somerset Yeomanry/44th RTR.
The Northumberland Hussars	Northumberland	15/19th Hussars	1947–1967	cadre incorporated into The Royal Yeomanry Regiment in 1971
40th (The King's) Royal Tank Regiment	Liverpool	1st RTR	1947–1956	amalgamated with 41st (Oldham) Royal Tank regiment to form 40th/41st RTR
41st (Oldham) Royal Tank Regiment	Oldham	3rd RTR	1947–1956	amalgamated with 40th (The King's) Royal Tank regiment to form 40th/41st RTR
42nd (7th (23rd London Btn) The East Surrey Regt) RTR	London	8th RTR	1947–1956	converted to infantry 23rd London Bt, East Surrey Regiment
43rd (6th(City) Battalion, The Royal Northumberland Fusiliers) Royal Tank Regiment	Newcastle	7th RTR	1947–1956	disbanded and remustered as infantry
44th/50th Royal Tank Regiment	Bristol	5th RTR	1947–1956	amalgamated with North Somerset Yeomanry
45th/51st (Leeds Rifles) Royal Tank Regiment	Yorkshire	6th RTR	1947–1958	converted to infantry The Prince of Wales's Own Regiment of Yorkshire
The Nottinghamshire Yeomanry (Sherwood Rangers Yeomanry) and after 1951 The Sherwood Rangers Yeomanry	Nottingham	17th/21st Lancers	1947–1992	Absorbed into The Royal Yeomanry

Territorial Army Regiment, RAC	Recruitment Area	Regular army affiliation	Years active (RAC role)	Notes
The Scottish Horse	Scotland	The Royal Scots Greys	1947–1956	amalgamated with The Fife and Forfar Yeomanry to form The Fife and Forfar Yeomanry/Scottish Horse
The Shropshire Yeomanry	Shropshire	4th Queen's Own Hussars	1947–1967	converted to Infantry, raised from cadres in 1971 as part of Mercian Yeomanry
The Staffordshire Yeomanry	Staffordshire	16th/5th Lancers	1947–1967	converted to Infantry, raised from cadres in 1971 as part of Mercian Yeomanry
The Warwickshire Yeomanry	Warwickshire	13th/18th Hussars	1947–1969	absorbed from cadres into Mercian Yeomanry
The Westminster Dragoons	London	2nd RTR	1947–1961	Amalgamated with Berkshire Yeomanry (RA) and Queen's Own Oxfordshire Hussars to form Berkshire and Westminster Dragoons
The Royal Wiltshire Yeomanry (The Prince of Wales's Own)	Wiltshire	The 10th Hussars	1947–1967	absorbed into Royal Yeomanry 1967, disbanded and raised from cadre in 1971 to form part of The Royal Wessex Yeomanry
The Yorkshire Hussars	Yorkshire	8th King's Royal Irish Hussars	1947–1956	amalgamated with the Queen's Own Yorkshire Dragoons and the East Riding Yeomanry to form the Queen's Own Yorkshire Yeomanry
The Queen's Own Yorkshire Dragoons	Yorkshire	9th Lancers	1947–1956	amalgamated with the Yorkshire Hussars and the East Riding Yeomanry to form the Queen's Own Yorkshire Yeomanry
The Berkshire and Westminster Dragoons	London and Berkshire	2nd RTR	1961–1967	absorbed into The Royal Yeomanry
The North Somerset Yeomanry/44th RTR	West Midlands	3rd RTR and 5th RTR	1956–1967	renamed the North Somerset and Bristol Yeomanry 1965
40th/41st Royal Tank Regiment	Liverpool and Manchester area	1st RTR	1956–1967	absorbed into Duke of Lancaster's Own Yeomanry
The Queen's Own Lowland Yeomanry	Scotland	The Royal Scots Greys until 1969, thereafter SCOTS DG	1956–1969	converted to fuel tanker squadron RASC

Territorial Army Regiment, RAC	Recruitment Area	Regular army affiliation	Years active (RAC role)	Notes
The Leicestershire and Derbyshire Yeomanry	Leicestershire and Derbyshire	9th/12th Lancers	1957–1969	became part of TA element Royal Anglian Regiment
The Queen's Own Yorkshire Yeomanry	Yorkshire	13th/18th Hussars and 4th/7th Royal Dragoon Guards	1956–1969	disbanded 1969, raised from cadre in 1971 to form part of the Queen's Own Yeomanry
Berkshire and Westminster Dragoons	London, Berkshire	2nd RTR	1961–1969	transferred Royal Signals 1969
Kent and County of London Yeomanry (Sharpshooters)	London	1st The Royal Dragoons until 1969, The Blues and Royals thereafter	1961–1967, raised again 1973	became part of The Royal Yeomanry in 1973.
Duke of Lancaster's Own Yeomanry (Royal Tank Regiment)	Lancashire	14th/20th Hussars, The Royal Tank Regiment	1967–1992	affiliation with RTR ended in 1969. amalgamated with Queen's Own Mercian Yeomanry
The Royal Yeomanry Regiment	Berkshire, London, Wiltshire, Nottinghamshire, Kent, Northern Ireland	By Squadron (1)	1967–present	raised from The Berkshire and Westminster Dragoons, The Royal Wiltshire Yeomanry, The Sherwood Rangers Yeomanry, The Kent and County of London Yeomanry and The North Irish Horse as component squadrons
The Queens Own Mercian Yeomanry	Warwickshire, Worcestershire, Shropshire, Staffordshire	By Squadron (2)	1971–1992	raised from cadres of Warwickshire, Shropshire, Staffordshire and Worcestershire Yeomanries that stood down in 1969. Amalgamated with the Duke of Lancaster's Own Yeomanry in 1992.
The Queen's Own Yeomanry (2nd Armoured Car Regiment)	Yorkshire, Cheshire, Scotland, Northumberland	By Squadron (3)	1971–present	raised from cadres of Cheshire Yeomanry, Queens Own Yorkshire Yeomanry, Ayrshire Yeomanry and Northumberland Hussars stood down in 1969.
The Wessex Yeomanry	West Midlands and South West	By Squadron (4)	1971–present	formed from cadres of Royal Gloucestershire Hussars, Royal Wiltshire Yeomanry, The Royal Devon Yeomanry
(1) HQ Sqn: Berkshire and Westminster Dgns, A Sqn: R. Wiltshire Yeo. B Sqn: Sherwood Rangers, C Sqn: Kent and Sharpshooters, D Sqn: North Irish Horse	(2) HQ Sqn: A Sqn: Warwickshire and Worcestershire Yeo, B Sqn: Staffs Yeo, C Sqn: Shropshire Yeo	(3) HQ Sqn: Northumberland H., A Sqn: Ayrshire Yeo, C Sqn: Cheshire Yeo, Y Sqn: Yorkshire Yeo	(4) A Sqn: R. Glos. H., B Sqn: R. Wiltshire Yeo, C Sqn: R. Glos. H D Sqn R. Devon Yeo	

Appendix II

RAC Battle Tanks 1945–1990

Type	Comet Mk.I	Centurion Mk.I	Centurion Mk.3	Centurion Mk.7 and Mk.8	Centurion Mk.11, Mk.12 and Mk.13	Conqueror Mk.1 and Mk.2	Chieftain Mk.2	Chieftain Mk.5	Chieftain Mk.11	Challenger I Mk.2
weight	32.7 tons	50 tons	52 tons	52 tons	52 tons	65 tons	54 tons	54 tons	55 tons	62 tons
crew	5	4	4	4	4	4	4	4	4	4
main armament	77mm Mk.II	17 pounder	20pounder	20 pounder	105mm	120mm rifled L1	120mm L11A3-5	120mm L11A3-5	120mm L11A3-5	120mm L11A3-5
co-axial armament	7.92mm Besa	7.92mm Besa*	7.92mm Besa	.30 Browning	.30 Browning	.30 Browning	7.62 GPMG	7.62 GPMG	7.62 GPMG	7.62 GPMG
cupola armament	no	no	no	.30 Browning	.30 Browning	.30 Browning	7.62 GPMG	7.62 GPMG	7.62 GPMG	7.62 GPMG
max. armour turret front	102mm	120mm	152mm	152mm	152mm	200mm	195mm	195mm	195mm + applique	Classified Chobham
max. armour hull front	76mm	57mm	76mm	76mm	120mm	130mm	120mm	120mm	120mm	Classified Chobham
max. armour turret sides	63mm	76mm	90mm	90mm	90mm	89mm	80mm	80mm	80mm	Classified
max. armour hull sides	44mm	51mm	51mm	51mm	51mm	40mm	38mm	38mm	38mm	Classified
armour turret rear	63mm	76mm	90mm	90mm	90mm	70mm	50mm	50mm	50mm	Classified
armour hull rear	31mm	35mm	35mm	35mm	35mm	38mm	30mm	30mm	30mm	Classified
engine	Meteor Mk.VIII	Meteor IVB	Meteor IVB	Meteor IVB	Meteor IVB	Meteor M120/fuel injected	Leyland L60	Leyland L60	Leyland L60	Perkins CV-12

Type	Comet Mk.I	Centurion Mk.I	Centurion Mk.3	Centurion Mk.7 and Mk.8	Centurion Mk.11, Mk.12 and Mk.13	Conqueror Mk.1 and Mk.2	Chieftain Mk.2	Chieftain Mk.5	Chieftain Mk.11	Challenger 1 Mk.2
power to weight ratio hp/ton	18 bhp/ton	13bhp/tonne	13bhp/tonne	13bhp/tonne	13bhp/tonne	12hp/tonne	11.9hp/tonne	11.9hp/tonne	11.9hp/tonne	19 hp/tonne
fuel type	petrol	petrol	petrol	petrol	petrol	petrol	multi fuel	multi fuel	multi fuel	Diesel
range on internal fuel	125 miles	100 miles	100 miles	200 miles	200 miles	100 miles	312 miles	312 miles	312 miles	280 miles
maximum gun range (direct)	800-1000 yds	800-1000 yds	1200-1400 yds	1200-1400 yds	3000 yds	8,500 yds	8,500 yds	8,500 yds	8,500 yds	8,500 yds
maximum practical FCS range	1400 yds	1400 yds	3000 yds	3000 yds	3000 yds	3,800 yds	3,800 yds	3,800 yds	3,800 yds	3,800 yds
Fire Control System	optical sights	optical sights	optical sights	ranging gun	ranging gun	early hunter/killer	Ranging gun	Laser	IFCS	IFCS
Night Vision Systems	no	no	no	no	yes	no	yes	yes	TOGS	TOGS
ammunition load gun/mg	62/5175	64/4250	64/4250	68/4500	68/4500	35/6000	53/6000	53/6000	53/6000	64/4000
maximum speed (road)	32 mph	21mph	21mph	21mph	21mph	21.5mph	25mph	25mph	25mph	35mph
maximum speed (cross country)	15mph	10mph	10mph	10mph	10mph	8/15mph	12mph	12mph	12mph	13mph
standard wireless	No.19	No19	No19	Larkspur	Larkspur	No 19	Larkspur	Clansman	Clansman	Clansman
years in service	1944-1960	1945-1955	1949-1974	1955-1974	1964-1974	1955-1966	1966-1989	1970-1989	1966-1989	1983/2001

Appendix III

RAC Middle East

RAC deployments Mediterranean and Middle East 1946–1990

Regiment				
9th Queen's Royal Lancers	Italy May 45–Oct46	Palestine Apr 47–Aug 47		
7th Queen's Own Hussars	Italy May 45–May46			
2nd Queen's Bays	Italy May 45–Jun 47	Egypt Jun 47–Sep 47	Jordan Dec 54–Feb 56	Libya Feb 56–Jul 57
1st King's Dragoon Guards	Palestine Sep 45–Dec 46	Libya Jan 47–Feb 48		
3rd The King's Own Hussars	Palestine Oct 45–Jan 48			
15th/19th The King's Royal Hussars	Egypt Oct 45–Dec 45	Palestine Dec 45–Oct 47	Sudan Nov 47–Mar 49	
2nd Royal Tank Regiment	Italy Dec 45–Sep 46			
4th Royal Tank Regiment	Italy Jan 46–Jul 47	Egypt Canal Zone, Palestine, Kuwait, Jordan Jun 47–Dec 52		
4th/7th Royal Dragoon Guards	Egypt Apr 46–Jun 46	Palestine Jun 46–Jun 48	Libya Jun 48–Oct 52	
8th Royal Tank Regiment	Egypt and Palestine May 46–Jul 47			
Life Guards	Egypt Jun 46–May 47	Palestine Jun 47–May 48	Egypt Jan 54–Dec 55	
12th (Prince of Wales's) Royal Lancers	Palestine Aug 46–Mar 47	Cyprus May 59–Jan 60		Cyprus Jul 55–Mar 56 (det. Sqn)
6th Royal Tank Regiment	Egypt Jul 47–Jan 48	Egypt (Suez) Nov 56–Jan 57	Libya, Jordan, Cyprus Nov 56–Sep 59 (det Sqns)	

RAC deployments Mediterranean and Middle East 1946–1990

Regiment				
13th/18th Royal Hussars (Queens Mary's Own)	Libya Feb 48–Jan 50	Egypt Jan 50–Apr 50 (A Sqn)	Egypt Apr–May 50	
16th/5th Lancers	Egypt Canal Zone Mar 48–Jan 51	Libya Feb 51–Apr 53	Sudan Jan 53–Apr 53 (A Sqn)	
1st The Royal Dragoons	Egypt Feb 51–Jan 54			
Royal Scots Greys	Libya Apr 52–May 55			
14th/20th King's Hussars	Libya Nov 52–Oct 55	Libya Dec 62–Dec 66		
5th Royal Inniskilling Dragoon Guards	Egypt Canal Zone Jan 53–Dec 53	Libya Sep 63–Oct 63	Libya Apr 64–Dec 64 (A Sqn)	Libya Dec 65–Nov 67 (Less A Sqn)
5th Royal Tank Regiment	Libya Dec 54- Feb 57	Libya Feb 65–Mar 65		
Royal Horse Guards (The Blues)	Cyprus Feb 56–Apr 59			
10th Royal Hussars (Prince of Wales Own)	Jordan Oct 56–Jul 57			
2nd Royal Tank Regiment	Libya Sep 59–Oct 61			
11th Hussars (Prince Albert's Own)	Kuwait Jun 61–Aug 61			
3rd Carabiniers (Prince of Wales's Dragoon Guards) (less B Sqn)	Kuwait Jul 61–Oct 61 (less B Sqn)	Libya Jan 68–Sep 68 (C Sqn)	Libya Sep 68–Jun 69 (B Sqn)	

RAC Asian Deployments

RAC deployments Asia 1948–1974

Regiment	Station	Arrival	Departure
3rd Royal Tank Regiment	Hong Kong and Malaya	Jul–49	Mar–52
8th King's Royal Irish Hussars	Korea	Oct–50	Dec–51
5th Royal Inniskilling Dragoon Guards	Korea	Dec–51	Dec–52
4th Queen's Own Hussars	Malaya	Sep–48	Sep–51
13th/18th Royal Hussars (Queen Mary's Own)	Malaya	Jun–50	Jul–53
7th Royal Tank Regiment (C Sqn)	Korea	Nov–50	Oct–51
13th/18th Royal Hussars (Queen Mary's Own) (B Sqn)	Hong Kong	Sep–51	Jul–53
12th Royal Lancers	Malaya	Sep–51	Jul–54
7th Royal Tank Regiment	Hong Kong	Feb–52	Oct–54
1st Royal Tank Regiment	Korea	Dec–52	Dec–53
11th Hussars (Prince Albert's Own)	Malaya and Singapore	Jul–53	Jul–56
5th Royal Tank Regiment	Korea	Nov–53	Nov–54
15th/19th the King's Royal Hussars	Malaya	Jul–54	Apr–56
7th Queen's Own Hussars	Hong Kong	Aug–54	Aug–57
1st King's Dragoon Guards	Malaya	Jun–56	Aug–58
1st Royal Tank Regiment	Hong Kong	Jun–57	Mar–60
13th/18th Royal Hussars (Queen Mary's Own)	Malaya	Jul–58	Dec–60
1st The Royal Dragoons	Malaysia and Singapore	Dec–60	Sep–62
Queen's Royal Irish Hussars	Malaysia and Brunei	Oct–62	Jan–64
16th/5th The Queen's Royal Lancers (A Sqn)	Hong Kong	Nov–63	Dec–64
Queen's Royal Irish Hussars	Borneo	Jan–64	Sep–64
5th Royal Inniskilling Dragoon Guards (C Sqn)	Hong Kong	Dec–64	Dec–65
4th Royal Tank Regiment	Malaysia, Borneo, Singapore, Brunei	Aug–64	Sep–66
1st Queen's Dragoon Guards (B Sqn + Air Sqn)	Borneo	Feb–65	Aug–65
1st Queen's Dragoon Guards (C Sqn + Air Sqn)	Borneo	Aug–65	Feb–66
Life Guards	Malaysia and Borneo	Sep–65	Oct–68
5th Royal Tank Regiment (H Sqn)	Borneo	Feb–66	Sep–66
Queen's Own Hussars (A+ C Sqn)	Singapore and Hong Kong	Oct–68	Aug–70
14th/20th King's Hussars (Sqns detached to Cyprus, Northern Ireland and Tidworth)	Singapore and Hong Kong	Jun–70	May–73
16th/5th The Queen's Royal Lancers (C Sqn)	Hong Kong	May–73	Oct–74